The American
COCKER SPANIEL

The American
COCKER

SPANIEL

Dr. Alvin Grossman

Sun City, Arizona
2000

Published by Doral Publishing, Sun City, Arizona
Printed in the United States of America.

Copyedited by Lisa Liddy
Book Design/Typesetting by The Printed Page
Cover by Michael Allen

Library of Congress Card Number: 00-100753
ISBN: 0-944875-59-9

Top Producing Cocker of All Time
CH. EMPIRE'S BROOKLYN DODGER
Breeder: Jeff Wright

Contents

Acknowledgments xi
Chapter 1. A History 1
Chapter 2. The American Spaniel Club 11
Chapter 3. The Golden Era The First Peak of Popularity 19
Chapter 4. The Golden Era Resurgence of the Breed 29
Chapter 5. Form Follows Function 33
    Organic Engineering 34
    Movement 36
    Simple Bio-Machines 37
    Hydraulics and Life 38
    Organic Architecture (Type) 39
    Structure, Shape and Symmetry 39
Chapter 6. General Appearance—The Standard of the Breed 41
    Size, Proportion, Substance 41
    Size 41
    Proportion 42
    Head 42
    Neck, Topline, Body 43
    Forequarters 43
    Hindquarters 44
    Coat 44
    Color and Markings 44
    Gait 45
    Temperament 46
    Disqualifications 46
Chapter 7. They Come In Coats of Many Hues 47
    Blacks 47
    Buffs 51
    Chocolates 56
    Bi-Colors 73
    Parti-Colors 77
    Tri-Colors 82
    Mismarks 87

Chapter 8. The Versatile Cocker As a Show Dog **91**
  Introduction 93
    Early Socialization Important 93
    Table Training 95
    Posing 96
    Lead Training 104
    Sitting 108
    Sidewinding 108
    Temperament 109
    Grooming 111
Chapter 9. The Versatile Cocker As An Obedience Dog **119**
    Dog Training Manuals 131
    Kennels and Schools 131
    The Private Trainer 132
    The Group Obedience Class 133
Chapter 10. The Versatile Cocker As A Hunting Dog **139**
Chapter 11. Outstanding Breeders and Kennels **157**
Chapter 12. Dogs Who Influenced the Breed **173**
Chapter 13. Great Winning Dogs of the Recent Past **201**
Chapter 14. Great Winning Bitches of the Recent Past **213**
Chapter 15. Top Producing Dogs **221**
Chapter 16. Top Producing Bitches **227**
Chapter 17. How The Dog Show Game Works **233**
Bibliography **241**
    Periodicals 241
    Books 242
Index **243**

Acknowledgments

The author would like to thank the American Spaniel Club for its kind permission to use material from two important bodies of work. From a *Century of Spaniels Volume I*, I have utilized the excellent work of Dr. Francis Greer in detailing the history of the Spaniel Club. The Spaniel Club has also graciously granted me permission to use the material from the new slide/tape presentation of the standard and Ralph Craig's field training manual.

The American Kennel Club has also granted permission to use the slide/tape material.

B & E Publications has given kind permission to quote extensively from Frank Sabella and Shirlee Kalstone in their book *The Art of Handling Show Dogs*.

To the editors of *Akita World* magazine, many thanks for permission to use several parts of various issues concerning kennel management.

To Michael Allen, former editor of the *American Cocker Magazine* for permission to use numerous quotes both of my work and others from a variety of issues.

To Lynn Lowy, former editor and publisher of the *Great Dane Reporter*, many thanks for permission to use significant material from a number of issues.

To Susan Coe, editor of *The Basenji*, for granting permission to use special material for this text.

To Joe McGinnis, of Doll/McGinnis Publications, for kind permission to use material from a variety of magazines they publish.

To Marie Tayton, widow of Mark Tayton, for permission to quote from his book *Successful Kennel Management*.

I would like to acknowledge the use of statistics on top producers gleaned from Irene Castle Schlintz's two volumes of *Top Producing Spaniels* as well as the contribution of Dr. Marge Saari without whose help the ranking and producing records would not be possible.

Many thanks to J.B. Lippincott Company for permission to quote from *The Human Pedigree* by Anthony Smith.

Permission has been granted by Donald Stutz, Jr. Editor/Publisher of the *Golden Retriever Review*, to use specific material from various issues.

American Sporting Dogs, edited by Eugene V. Connett and published by D. Van Nostrand Company, Inc. is the source of much of the material on scent in hunting dogs.

CHAPTER 1

A History

Anthony Smith, in his treatise *The Human Pedigree*, points out a study of ancient history. He taught us:

> All the main groups of dogs were created long before Christ had appeared. In fact, they already existed when written history was making its first appearance, and when their various canine shapes and sizes were being made readily recognizable on stone and pottery. The breeding of dogs is extremely ancient, and modern breeders (who held their first dog show—in England at Newcastle—in 1859) have added little, whatever they may think, to the work done by the end of the Neolithic period of history.
>
> There are several points of interest in dog evolution. First, although these animals are still happily able to identify one of their own kind, there has been tremendous variation in dog variety. There is curly hair, straight hair, wiry hair, silky hair, long faces, compressed faces, floppy ears, erect ears. There is a world of difference in the tail alone. As for weight, the Chihuahua can be confronted by Mastiffs forty times their size. Second, the bulk of this differentiation has been caused by man, deliberately and for different purposes. Man has controlled their random mating and has demonstrated the extraordinary variability inherent in the species (for it is just one species). Natural selection tends normally to enforce a greater uniformity among individuals, but given artificial selection or the artificial world of cohabitating with man, this variability can express itself.

We know from a reading of history that when men were banding together to form large village communities, they brought their dogs with them. Since then, both have experienced in similar fashion the cultural and environmental changes that have occurred-canned food, heated rooms, soft furnishings, urban compression, disease control, and increasing unnaturalness. At the same time, dogs with their quicker breeding cycle have passed through some 400 generations, while man has experienced a tenth of that number. It is these facts, according to Marsha A. Burns and Margaret N. Fraser in *Genetics of the Dog*, an excellent book on dog behavior, which suggest a hypothesis: "The genetic consequences of civilized living have been intensified in the dog, and therefore the dog should give us some idea of the genetic future of mankind...In short, the dog may be a genetic pilot experiment for the human race."

There is one further important point. Evolution, or rapid genetic change, happens fastest when a population is divided into small isolated groups that have only occasional genetic contact with each other. (In American Cockers that was precisely what was happening in pre-World War II America. Travel was very limited, so not many dogs were shipped any great distance to be bred. As a result, there grew to be a "western type" with long sloping shoulders, a steeper topline, and with finer bone which did not fully develop until about two years of age. On the opposite coast the style was different. The "eastern type" had a blockier head, was straighter and heavier through the shoulders, had a shorter back and more coat. With the advent of regular commercial air travel, the Cocker has been largely homogenized.) According to Smith, this was precisely the condition of mankind 10,000 years ago, when dogs were becoming a part of each isolated scene. The trading, or warring, or friendly association between each group permitted a degree of genetic involvement with the dogs next door. For instance, with living areas spaced well apart, American Indians each had their own breed of dog. These breeds were not greatly different from those of each neighboring tribe, but across the continent the differences became intense. So, too, in earlier times-with all the fairly isolated, semi-independent groups of people that were the ancestors of us all.

John C. McLoughlin, writing in *The Canine Clan*, agrees with Smith that during the Neolithic time in history mankind took off in its present direction. The various breeds of dog were dotted everywhere. They had been nurtured in isolation and were then ready to accompany their migrating masters, to be sold or captured along the way. It is interesting to note that practically every dog name is based upon the geographical area from which that creature had arrived. The spotted dog, for example, may not have originated in Dalmatia (in fact it was India) but it came through there, and that was good enough for its new owners; so too, with the Spaniel (allegedly Espagnol), the Greyhounds (allegedly Greek), the Saluki (thought to be Seleucid).

As the age of discovery began, man's movements became more frenetic. No longer did small groups wander along conventional lines, but boatloads leapfrogged among the continents. Everyone took dogs with them, and they brought dogs back. There was much *panmixis*, or widescale interbreeding. Sometimes this was successful, sometimes not. New breeds were formed, often at the expense of native varieties that died out, as in America and South Africa.

The American Cocker Spaniel is a perfect example of this *panmixis* in modern times. In the middle 1880's there was a degree of confusion over some of the Spaniels. The base dog was called a Field Spaniel. He tended to be a large dog. Smaller Spaniels, even ones from the same litter, were called Cockers and shown in a different class. Gradually, the Sussex, and Field Spaniels drifted away. And the Cocker, which had been imported to America, became a big hit. He drew from the best of the base Spaniels and left them in his wake. Today, Sussex and Field Spaniels in this country struggle for survival while the is a top ranked dog in American Kennel Club (AKC) registrations. After the turn of the century, Cockers in the United States were of English type and American type. In fact one of the pillars of the American Cocker breed has an English Cocker dam. They were shown as one breed.

Finally, in the 1950's, Mrs. Geraldine Dodge, a patron of the English Cocker conducted a thorough pedigree study which convinced the AKC to grant the English Cocker status as an independent breed.

The *Canidae* (the family of Dog) itself was derived, at least in historical terms, fairly recently. They came from more primitive and ancestral predators. They fanned out rapidly into different regions but never lost their ability to adapt. They evolved in a direction that would permit them a wider selection of food options available from the world's ecosystems. They could survive by eating various vegetable foods in addition to flesh. The wild carnivore was not rigidly tied to the condition of any one food chain position and very nearly approaches man in dietary adaptability. Among the *Canidae* were the wolves (*Canis lupus*), a species having much in common with early man, that exhibited cooperative behavior when attacking its prey. The *Canidae* expresses in form and function an ancestral invasion of open country, wherein prey must be hunted by tireless running rather than by stalking. Reading *The Canine Clan* certainly indicates wolf and man were direct competitors, and this similarity of life style may have had much to do with their eventual union. From the study of archeology and related sciences, it is known that all modern dogs derive only from the various races of the wolf species and that the association of wolf and man leading to dog happened again and again. American Indians were frequently accustomed to taking wolf cubs, either to amend their dog stock or to start afresh. Probably this process of turning wolves into dogs was spurred on when man's extreme inability to smell out his prey, in that tangle of hiding places, became a terrible disadvantage.

The mighty sense of smell in *canids* may be illustrated by the fact, (experimentally shown) that a dog can detect, for example, the odor of fear in the urine of another which has long since passed by, and thus be on the lookout for trouble in advance. *Canids* are aided in their sense of smell by a pair of small openings, Jacobsen's organs, in the front of the roof of the mouth. Using these, a *canid* "tastes" the air as he smells it, curling his lips to do so in a motion referred to by the German word *flehmen*. In *flehmen*, the animal raises his nose, wrinkles his snout, and ceases breathing, while he bares his fore-teeth and samples the air with his Jacobsen's organs. In a later chapter on training the Cocker for the field, it should be noted that major emphasis is placed on this smelling ability.

Anyway, as Smith points out:

> *The dog, a remarkable social invention, was the first domestic animal. The new accomplice could be tamed, if caught early enough or reared in human company. It could hunt. It could herd animals. It could protect and give warning, although wild Canidae are not given to protective barking as much as the tame varieties. Each tribe must have wanted this new aid to living, and good bitches must have been tremendously in demand.*
>
> *However, a good forest dog is not necessarily suitable either for the open plains, or for herding semi-domestic stock, or for guarding*

the encampments. Therefore, there had to be selective breeding for specific purposes. Therefore, there evolved hunting dogs, sheep dogs, and even the "toy" dogs of the Maltese type. Living with the early Egyptians there were at least five major kinds: the Basenji, the Grey-hound, the Maltese, the Mastiff, and a sort of Chow.

It is important to appreciate that the changes, however striking, were not basic. They were more of degree of proportion. Of course, dogs also differ in those characteristics that were different even in the basic wolf, such as: color, temperament, and wiriness, smoothness or furriness of hair.

A large number of dog differences are the result of the retention of juvenile features. This occurs when any creature stops growing or achieves its adult state while still possessing characteristics previously associated with its more immature form. Puppies, for example, have silkier, less wavy hair. Their ears, in general, are floppier, less straight, and less erect than with the adult. Their tails are more likely to droop, less likely to stay firmly away from the legs. There is no law that states that these features must be linked with the juvenile form, but some of the dog changes have inclined toward these puppylike features. (Many of the Pekingese characteristics are an example.)

Early man lived in different environments, therefore, his dog requirements differed from place to place. These have also changed in more recent times, and the breeders have had to adapt the supply. The pet or toy breeds, suitable for living within a household, have been more favored. A 1987 study by AKC indicated that more small breeds have moved into the top 20 dogs in registration, led of course by the American Cocker with nearly 100,000 registered each year.

In the early Aztec world, dogs were bred for eating, for their hair (as wool), and for their role as beasts of burden. The whiteness of the English Terriers was a requirement for greater conspicuousness within the undergrowth. Even the arrival of breech-loading guns demanded a different animal; the steadfast and entirely patient behavior of the pointing breeds, doggedly stationary while his master fulfilled the ritual of preparing a muzzle-loader, was far too steadfast when a more capable firing piece became available. Therefore, Setters were deliberately bred from Spaniel stock (the English primarily) to sit or "set" when the quarry was detected and then to move forward when the quicker gun was ready. As the gun became better, the Spaniel—who worked close in flushing game—became more of a favorite.

In short, different dogs have been our steady requirement. The breeders (whether putting their animals out at night to be mated by wolves, or actively preventing such an event, or trading particular animals up and down the migration routes) have always been attempting to satisfy most particular needs. Smith indicated that during the past 20,000 years these men have been outstandingly successful in unleashing the potential variation in the domestic dog—the animal that once was a wolf.

Not only have physical characteristics been selected for; behavior has always been important. The breeder has had to provide an animal's ferocity (guard dogs), or overall friendliness (Cocker Spaniels), or individual friendliness (loyalty to one person alone). There is, for example, the matter of barking. Some individual dogs bark more than others; some breeds do. It can even be proved (in *Animal Behavior*, John Paul Scott and John L. Fuller have done so) that this behavioral trait has a genetic basis.

For their experiment they took the Basenji, a poor barker, and the Cocker Spaniel, a sometimes noisy creature.

> *Basenjis is not only bark rarely, but make less noise when they do and stop quicker when they start. Presumably the barking facility served less purpose in the African forests, or the barker was pounced on more readily by dog-loving leopards. Whether their masters selected them for their quietness or whether leopards saved them the trouble, the modern examples of this breed howl or yowl more than they bark. Any kind of howl, with its wavering note, is harder to locate and pinpoint than the bark. The Cocker, on the other hand, named after its ability to flush out woodcock, is a standard barker. Given a form of incentive to do so, the Cockers barked, during the experiment, on 68 percent of these occasions. The Basenji not only barked less loudly and more briefly when subjected to similar stimuli, but responded on only 20 percent of the occasions.*

As of now, the tendency toward diversity has gone to greater lengths in dog than in man for two reasons. First, natural selection for the dog has been relaxed for a longer time-in terms of generations—than for man. Second, artificial selection—of the dog by man—has deliberately preserved some unwelcome canine mutations merely to increase that diversity. Has the dog species therefore suffered genetically? Natural selection is impartial, favoring no species in particular, but has its lack of influence caused some kind of lack and unfitness in the dog?

> *The answer is that the dog does not seem to be genetically weak. For example, the current breeds are largely more fertile than their wolf ancestors. Wolves mature at the age of two and produce four or five cubs per litter. There may be selective reasons for this casual growth, such as the inability of the habitat to support large numbers of predators, but the wolfs infertility is still the case. The dog is, generally speaking, sexually mature before the age of one and can produce two litters a year. By this criterion, man-handling has not harmed the dog.*

Nor has it in the range of capabilities. Variety is the keynote, and today's dogs have broadened all the old wolf characteristics. "Terriers," to quote Scott and Fuller again, "are more aggressive than their wolf forebears; the hound breeds less so. Greyhounds are faster than wolves; short-legged dogs, like the Dachshund, less so. The good scent dogs are better trackers than wolves, while terriers are poorer. Sheep dogs can herd more effectively; other breeds would not know where to begin. Many game dogs are, reasonably enough, more interested than wolves in game and share man's enthusiasm about birds."

American Cockers originally belonged to a large family of animals that assumed a wide variety of sizes, shapes and colors. Over time, they aligned themselves into two distinct groups, land Spaniels and water Spaniels. Members of the land Spaniels group include the American Cocker, the English Cocker, the English Springer, the Sussex and the Welsh Springer. The water group consists of the Irish Water Spaniel and the American Water Spaniel. At one time, there was an English Water Spaniel in the water group and a Norfolk Spaniel in the land group. But these have disappeared from this country over the last fifty years. Also, at one time, Toy Spaniels were a part of the land group.

According to Ella B. Moffit in her book *The Cocker Spaniel*, "Spaniels, until the middle of the 19th century, were classified according to size of the individual dog. In England, it was not until 1883 that classes for Cockers were listed in shows, and not until 1893 that the English Kennel Club granted the Cocker Spaniel a place for himself in the Stud Book. In the last quarter of the 19th century, the Cocker lost his place in the field

Ch. Obo II, 1882

to the English Springer. It was evident that the long and low-set dog that Cockers had become (bred for those exaggerations, then considered beautiful), was responsible for their fall from grace as a field dog supreme. We do owe a debt of gratitude to those breeders of yore for having established a definite strain which is the foundation of our Cockers of today. However, the contrast between Champion Obo II of 1882 and the modern Cocker of 100 years later is astonishing. Obo, the sire of Obo II, bred by a Mr. Farrow, was whelped on June 14, 1879. He is recorded as being by 'Fred out of Betty.'" My, what might the AKC think if we attempted such simplicity?

According to Dalziell's *British Dogs*, Obo had the following measurements:

Weight	22 pounds
Height	10 inches
Length from nose to ears	2 ¼ inches
Length from nose to occiput	7 ¼ inches
Length from nose to set-on of tail	29 inches

Today, a typical American Cocker male would weigh nearly 30 pounds, be 14¾ to 15½ inches tall. This certainly shows the dramatic changes our breed has undergone.

Ch. Tagalong's Winter Frost, a top winner. Owned by Frank DeVito and Jose Serrano and pictured here with her handler, Wilson Pike.

It was in 1790 that one first finds reference in English literature to the Springing Spaniel and the Cocking Spaniel. The Cocking Spaniel was so small that today he would be put into the Toy group. His weight was estimated at between 11-16 pounds. Mrs. Moffit felt that it was inconceivable that a dog of that size should be valued for sport. In her opinion, their size could only be explained by the fact that they were used in numbers as noisy drivers. In the early 19th century, there is mention of them being used in conjunction with Greyhounds to spring the hare which the latter would course.

There is much in our breed history to learn. Many good books which contain historical data are to be found. I can especially recommend *The Complete Cocker Spaniel* by Milo Denlinger, published by Denlinger Publishers. This book is out of print but if you can find a copy—treasure it. Ella Moffit's book, *The Cocker Spaniel*, is also a gem. A later book, *The Cocker Spaniel*, by Norman Austin is also a valuable resource.

There is also a great deal of history of the breed to learn by perusing the section to appear later in this book entitled, "Dogs Who Influenced The Breed".

An artist's conception of an ideal Cocker Spaniel head

CHAPTER 2

The American Spaniel Club

One January afternoon in 1881, James Watson called at Clinton Wilmerding's office in New York City. The purpose of his visit was to suggest that they form a Spaniel Club.

Moving rapidly, the two men contacted other Spaniel lovers. In February, thirteen other charter members were present at the organizational meeting in addition to Watson and Wilmerding. Present were George McDougall (Watson's partner in Lachine Kennels); Dr. J.S. Niven, E. Tinsley, and J.F. Kirk from Canada; J. Otis Fellows, M.P. Mckoon, A.E. Goddefroy, Dr. J.S. Cattanack, Dr. J.L. Morrill, A.H. Moore, C.B. Cummings, J.H. Whitman, and A. McCollom. They named the new club the American Cocker Spaniel Club and elected Mr. Moore president.

First order of business was to draw up standards which would officially separate Cocker Spaniels and Field Spaniels. In England, small Field Spaniels were usually called "Cockers" by the breeders. But the English Kennel Club did not recognize Cockers as a separate breed until 1892, even though early dog shows frequently had classes for large Field Spaniels and small Field Spaniels.

It was difficult to draft these standards. Into them had to go a blending of opinions that would please and satisfy the majority. After all, a standard is a statement of intent and not a commandment from a higher source. Following months of compromises, disagreements, and reconciliations, the standards were completed. There was little difference between the two breeds except weight, height, and length. The Field Spaniel became proportionately heavier, lower, and longer than the Cocker. A Cocker could weigh between 18 and 28 pounds; the Field was over 28 and up to 45 pounds.

The length of a Cocker Spaniel "from tip of nose to root of tail should be twice the height at shoulder, rather more than less," according to the first standard. All colors to be acceptable, but "beauty of color and markings must be taken into consideration."

The physical characteristics that separated the two breeds were more semantic than real in the early days. For example, Ch. Compton Brahmin, a Cocker champion, sired Ch. Compton Bandit, a Field champion, out of a Cocker-sized bitch.

Not all members were happy with the standards. At the club's annual meeting in 1886, member Arthur E. Rendle made the motion that "Owing to the interbreeding of Cockers and Field Spaniels for years past, the two breeds are so mixed up that it would be advisable to call them all Field Spaniels, to be divided by weight—lightweight and heavyweight."

That motion lost, but Mr. Rendle persevered. He introduced the motion again in 1894, and again it was defeated. This was the last time in the history of the club that an effort was made to recombine the breeds.

After the American Kennel Club was formed, it accepted Field and Cocker Spaniels as separate breeds for show and championship purposes, but registered them together in the Stud Book. By 1905, the two breeds had become sufficiently divergent in type and ancestry for the AKC to separate them for registration.

After the purpose for founding the club had been accomplished, the name was changed to the American Spaniel Club and the members turned their attention to other activities. The enthusiasm of some was diminished, however, and the club came close to extinction before its fifth anniversary. Mr. Wilmerding recalled in an interview that the membership had dwindled to seven in 1885, and had a record of $35 in the treasury. In a reorganization move, Roger Hemingway was elected president and Mr. Wilmerding the secretary-treasurer. Mr. Wilmerding could account for the seven members, but as he said, "I never found the $35!"

Major activities of the club during the first 20 years included development of standards, selection of approved judges from its membership, inauguration of puppy sweepstakes, attempted organization of field trials, and struggling to keep itself financially sound. And lest one think that these early members were gentlemen without flaw or passion; they disagreed, they argued, charges and countercharges abounded. Mr. Wilmerding was the peacemaker, who soothed injured feelings and kept the club alive.

Cocker Spaniel, Clumber Spaniel, Field Spaniel
Circa 1919

Most American Spaniel Club members bred and hunted over Sussex, Clumber, and Irish Water Spaniels in addition to their Cocker and Field Spaniels. It was decided that these other breeds were also entitled to the support and protection of the club. The Irish Water Spaniel—established in type and performance many years before the club was formed—was adopted with the same standard as published in England. The Clumber Spaniel Standard as drawn up by its committee, was not accepted until a number of revisions were made. Mr. Wilmerding and Mr. F. Kitchell on the east coast, Mr. A.L. Weston of Denver, and Mr. F.H.Y. Mercer and Mr. Joseph Hill of Canada imported the blood of top English Clumbers to try to increase their numbers and quality in North America.

The Sussex Spaniel was almost orphaned a century ago. He had nearly been lost as a distinct breed in England, and was still in the process of attempted rejuvenation to his earlier magnificent stature as a sporting dog. Some Sussex were imported to North America but were entered in the Stud Book as Field and Cocker Spaniels. Three of the first Field Spaniel champions in the United States were imported animals with the purest Sussex pedigrees.

Mr. Wilmerding helped save the Sussex from extinction, although he regretted the crossbreeding of Sussex and other Spaniels. "This, however," he wrote, "may be overlooked when we realize the rarity of the breed and the difficulty and expense entailed in mating them so scattered." He made this plea to the club: "It seems better by far, that this much-neglected breed should receive the assistance of the Spaniel Club and, like the Cockers, the Springers (viz. Field Spaniels), and Clumbers, be brought into public notice and prominence through the effort of this club."

And so, the Sussex joined the American Spaniel Club. But it was well into the 20th century before they were registered and shown under that name. Five breeds had joined the club during its first 20 years. In the next 20 years, the English Springer Spaniel and the Welsh Springer Spaniel would follow into the ranks.

The American Spaniel Club, as a display of its eminence as a club, was justly proud of the sterling silver challenge cups awarded to each of its breed winners and best brace from each breed. Because the annual Spaniel show was far in the future; the all-breed shows at which the cups were awarded were decided a year in advance. Only some of the cups were awarded at each chosen show. The judge had to be a person duly approved and elected by the club and only ASC members were eligible to win a "leg" on the cup. For permanent possession, a cup had to be won five times by the same individual.

In those days an elegant cup cost between $25 and $35. The treasury seldom boasted a balance sufficient to buy such challenge cups. However, by soliciting the members for donations of $5 or more the necessary funds were raised. Excitement was in the air at the executive committee meeting of March 12, 1891, when a letter was read from Dr. N. Rowe of Chicago. Dr. Rowe offered the club a $100 sterling silver challenge cup to be awarded as the club saw fit provided it was offered first at Westminster in 1892.

This trophy was named the "American Field Trophy" and was the most expensive award in ASC records for many years. It was first offered at Westminster's 1892 show for Best American-Bred Spaniel.

Puppy sweepstakes for Cocker Spaniels and Field Spaniels were inaugurated in 1887. The entry fee was $3, and the money was divided as follows: 40% to winner, 30% to breeder of winner, 20% to second place, and 10% to third. The club donated an additional $20 to the winner. The sweepstakes contest continued until it gradually evolved into the annual Futurity for Cocker Spaniel puppies in 1923.

Field trials might seem to have been a natural outgrowth of the American Spaniel Club's activities, but such was not the case. In May, 1892, Mr. Wilmerding was appointed chairman of a committee to investigate sponsoring ASC field trials. No progress was made. By February, 1906, the committee was still stalemated. This inability to kindle member enthusiasm continued for another five years. In 1911, Mr. Wilmerding resigned his chairmanship and the executive committee dispensed with the field trial committee. It would be more than another decade before this facet of ASC activity would be realized.

During the time ASC was busy with its own affairs; the American Kennel Club was formed in 1884. You will note its founding was three years after the Spaniel Club's. During its first year, AKC it did not envision being a registration body. But this soon became necessary. In late 1887, the AKC issued a ruling affecting all dog breeders and exhibitors. This new rule was read at the American Spaniel Club's executive committee meeting in January, 1888. It was not well received! The following resolution was passed by the committee:

> *Whereas, the American Kennel Club has altered its rules so as to compel the registration of all dogs in the Club Stud Book, and*
>
> *Whereas, it is the opinion of the Committee of the American Spaniel Club that such action is detrimental to the best interests of dog breeding, apart from any consideration as to the wisdom of compulsory registration, and*
>
> *Whereas, the Committee believes that the members of the Club should have a voice in the decision of the question, it being one outside of the routine business of the Club management, it is hereby resolved, that the members be requested to vote on the following question: (viz) "Shall the Club funds be distributed at shows where compulsory registration is enforced?"*

The first mail vote recorded in the ASC history showed 44 ballots returned, 35 of which agreed that club funds should be withheld from shows requiring dogs to be registered. In this matter, the ASC was fighting a losing battle.

This slight misunderstanding with the American Kennel Club was resolved rather rapidly. When the AKC began to accept club memberships, it was moved and carried at the annual meeting of 1889, that "The Spaniel Club make application through its secretary, for admission to the American Kennel Club." In August 1889, it was moved and carried that, "Mr. James Watson be appointed as delegate to represent the American Spaniel Club at the meetings of the AKC—in case of the election of the Spaniel Club to that body." The Spaniel Club became a member later in that year.

The second 20 years of the American Spaniel Club saw dramatic increases in membership and its first specialty show in 1894. The "big name" kennels, that both bred and bought Cocker Spaniels in quantity, appeared on the scene during this period. Many more shows were held and it followed that many more Cocker Spaniels would become champions.

As the ASC matured as an organization it evolved, as many organizations of its time, as an eastern-dominated club of people with money and leisure time in control of the organization. This is not meant to be a "put down" of the influential people who controlled the ASC, but a simple statement of the way the world was in the 1920's and 30's. In fact, the ASC was looked upon as a well-run organization, putting on excellent shows which continued to grow in popularity.

As the Cocker rose to the Number One position in all of dogdom, and breeders from other parts of the country became involved in the activities of the club, the eastern domination began to be challenged. This was a period of large kennels, many with expert kennel managers in residence. These exhibitors of wealth and standing, dominated the club and were major winners in the show ring.

The executive committee, heeding the cries throughout the country for better representation within the club and for more prestigious shows in local areas, created the zone concept. For its time and place this became a stroke of genius.

The zone concept divided the country into four regions or zones (a fifth was added later). A new prestige show called, logically enough, the Zone Show was created. Clubs within a zone could make application to hold a Zone Show. Upon approval, the ASC would help to support the event financially and would assist the local club in the management of the show. Only one designated Zone Show could be held in a given zone each year. The winners of these events were featured prominently, along with the winners of the January ASC show, in the annual report.

Perhaps the wisest move by the executive committee was to have zone representatives sit as members of the newly-constituted Board of Directors. Much credit for this innovation should be given to Bart King, the editor of the *Cocker Spaniel Visitor*, the predominant breed magazine of the day. In his editorial column called "Thoughts While Shaving," Bart used to take the Spaniel Club to task for their narrow views. In turn, credit should also be given to the club for listening to its members.

Although the zone shows became popular, there was still a feeling among the fancy that it was a limited show—one that only brought out the best in that zone. Occasionally, a widely-campaigned dog from another area would be shown. But this only served to whet the appetite of local exhibitors to see more such specimens.

Throughout the first 80 some years of the club's existence, there had been only one BIG show: the New York City Show. The breeders distant from New York found it difficult and expensive to travel to New York, especially during the first week in January. The west coast was beginning to make noises about proper representation on the Board, until the mid 1960's, only Ralph Brown (a wealthy northern California lumberman) had sat on the Board.

By the early 1970's, sentiment was running deep in the west to move the annual Specialty show, or to rotate its location around the country. Capitalizing on that sentiment, Robert Walker (of California) ran as an alternate candidate and won the presidency over the nominating committee's choice. In office, he turned out to be the maverick he said he would be. He was not nominated for a second term. Once again he ran as an alternative candidate and was reelected. Although many considered his time in office disruptive, he was in part responsible for establishing the concept of the summer National which is now rotated among the five zones.

Following Walker, the office of the presidency was held by persons from Illinois, Kentucky, Texas and again California. The club also elected its first woman president, Jeannie Meister of California. The club had truly become national in outlook.

Fortunately, the leadership of the club has been in good hands since its beginnings. Faced with the drastic problem of congenital cataracts in the breed, a responsible board in the 1970's set up and still maintains a Health Registry for unafflicted dogs. Additional heritable problems have also been included in the Registry.

In response to the growing worldwide popularity of the Cocker, the position of Liaison to Foreign Breed Clubs was established in the 1970's.

The American Spaniel Club's history has been one of steadfast loyalty and, at times, dynamic leadership. It has grown from the original 15 members to well over 1600. The entries at its two premier shows have continued to climb, and being selected to officiate at an ASC event is indeed an honor for a judge. There are still new paths to carve and ways to strengthen the club, however, there is good reason to be proud of the American Spaniel Club.

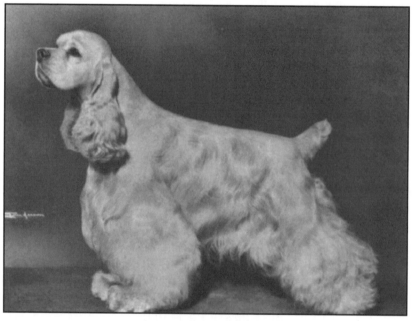

Ch. Carmor's Rise and Shine
Winner of Best in Show at Westminster

CHAPTER 3

The Golden Era
The First Peak of Popularity

The Cocker's first bid for popularity began in the early 1900's. From that time on, the golden era of America's Number One Sporting Dog flourished. In 1921, a Cocker Spaniel became the first of the breed to be named the winner of Best in Show at the Westminster Kennel Club. William T. Payne's Ch. Midkiff Seductive, a black and white Parti-Color, had this single honor. Not until 1940 and 1941 did another Cocker hold the spotlight at the Westminster Dog Show. The winner at that time was the famous Ch. My Own Brucie owned by the legendary Herman Mellenthin. In the 43 years that followed, only one other Cocker has topped that famous event—Ch. Carmor's Rise and Shine, handled by Ted Young, Jr.

In 1922, the Cocker Spaniel Breeder's Club of New England staged its first specialty show at Boston where W.T. Payne judged an entry of 106 dogs. Eight years later—in 1930—this same club ran up an unprecedented entry of 256 Cocker Spaniels. Only the "Shamrock" show held in Houston in 1951, and the Cocker Spaniel Club of Kentucky in 1986, had a larger entry (of course, this does not count ASC events). The 1930 show was judged by Mrs. A.R. Moffit, and was won by the Black bitch, Ch. My Own To-Day owned by the Windsweep Kennels of Miss Alice Dodsworth. My Own To-Day was of good size and essentially female in all details. Years later, Henry McTavey (one of the later breeders and judges of Cockers) stated that "Ch. My Own To-Day was the greatest dog-show Cocker up to that time."

Ch. My Own Brucie

Other winners of the New England specialty show were Ch. Luckknow Creme de la Creme, owned by Mr. and Mrs. Fred Brown; Ch. The Great My Own, property of Leonard Buck; the celebrated Ch. Idahurst Belle II carrying the banner of the O.B. Gilmans of Boston; Miss Dodsworth's Ch. Windsweep Ebony Boy; Ch. My Own Brucie, three times Best in Show, 1938, 1939, 1940; and Ch. Nonquitt Nola's Candidate, owned jointly by Mrs. Mildred Brister and Mrs. R.K. Cobb of Nanuet, New York. Oddly, the name of Ch. Torohill Trader, perhaps the greatest show dog of the time, does not appear on the roster.

The American Spaniel Club held its annual specialty at the Hotel Roosevelt in New York City until the 1970's. Starting in 1920, when Ch. Dunbar was Best in Show, the parent club's annual fixture grew in popularity. The greatest Cockers of the times were shown at the Roosevelt. Such names as Ch. Princess Marie, Ch. Midkiff Miracle Man, Sand Spring Storm Cloud, Ch. Windsweep Ladysman, Ch. Torohill Trader (1936 and 1937), Ch. My Own Brucie, Ch. Found, Ch. Nonquitt Nola's Candidate (1943 and 1945), and Ch. Try-Cob's Favorite Girl are some of the immortals who, in their year, wore the ermine robes.

The American Spaniel Club introduced the futurity stake in 1923, to encourage the breeding of better Cocker Spaniels. Bitches belonging to

Ch. Idahurst Belle II

Ch. Torohill Trader

Ch. Princess Marie

club members and due to whelp between February 1 and July 1 , were eligible for nomination in the futurity stake. This innovation was of tremendous popularity. The first futurity stake winner, and incidentally first for Mepal Kennels, was Mepal's Fortunata; second was Rees' Meteor, owned by Latimer Rees; third, was Mrs. W.M. Churchman's Jim Crow's Glow (bred by Dr. H.B. Kobler); and fourth was Sheila of Cassilis, owned by Cassilis Kennels.

Herman E. Mellenthin and his My Own Kennels, from Poughkeepsie, New York were beginning to be heard from in the 1930's. Mellenthin, a tall, soft-spoken man, took advantage of an offer of a free stud service to Robinhurst Foreglow. From this mating came the celebrated red Cocker, Red Brucie, a son of Foreglow and Ree's Dolly. Red Brucie never completed his championship, and wrote no show ring history. None, however, was needed to perpetuate his name, for the contribution of Red Brucie and his three half-brothers (all sons of Robinhurst Foreglow) propelled the Cocker Spaniel to the top of the AKC list of registrations in 1936. This truly opened the first golden era which lasted for some 16 years at which time, the Cocker was supplanted by the Beagle as the number one dog in America.

The names of the four sons of Foreglow, one or more of whom appeared in the pedigrees of most of the winning Cockers of the day, were Ch. Midkiff Miracle Man, Ch. Sand Spring Surmise, Ch. Limestone Laddie, and Red Brucie. In Red Brucie, Mellenthin had a dog that took him and his kennel to the heights.

Often called the "Wizard of Cockers," Mellenthin's contribution to the breed is preeminent. His home kennel, small and restricted, could not house all his bitches. Because of this, Mellenthin evolved a "farming out" system. Farmers of Duchess County were given bitches on breeding

Red Brucie

terms. Mellenthin was to pick the stud and to select his choice of the litter. At one time, Mellenthin had as many as 150 bitches farmed out. Naturally, breeding on this extensive scale gave Mellenthin a free hand in experimenting with bloodlines, crossing strains and breeding back to them, a thing no small breeder could hope to do.

Out of this experimentation came many of the greatest Cockers of the day. Ch. Torohill Trader, Ch. Princess Marie, Ch. My Own Again, Ch. My Own Straight Sale, Ch. My Own Brucie, Ch. The Great My Own, Ch. Merry Monarch of Falconhurst, Ch. Found and others too numerous to mention, were all the result of Mellenthin's breeding. It was not until after World War II that the Artru Kennels of Ruth and Art Benhoff would rival Mellenthin in producing such a string of great Cockers.

In the matter of Trader, the Torohill Kennels are the breeder of record, but it was Mellenthin who arranged the mating, who owned and later sold Trader to Leonard Buck's Blackstone Kennels.

A great deal of Mellenthin's success came from breeding back and into the Red Brucie strain. In addition to being a shrewd and intelligent breeder, Mellenthin was also a clever showman.

During this period Miss Alice Dodsworth purchased the Cordova Kennels and started to breed American-type Cockers. With such dogs as Ch. Coldstream Guard of Cordova, Ch. Cordova Cordial, Ch. Cordova Coccade, and with a dose of Mellenthin's advice, Miss Dodsworth's Windsweep Kennels soon swept to the pinnacle of success. In the 1930's, she introduced Ch. Windsweep Ladysman to the show ring. Ladysman, a Black dog of great refinement, became the top sire of his day. He died in 1944 and Miss Dodsworth had this to say about Ladysman and Mr. Mellenthin:

Ch. Windsweep Ladysman

"I like to hear good things said of my Ch. Windsweep Ladysman as I think he deserved them all. In his day he was a grand Cocker of real show and stud type, and in his old age he was game to the end.

"I miss him greatly...I lay my success to Red Brucie and to Ch. Coldstream Guard of Cordova and to Mr. Mellenthin's kindly advice..."

One of the great confrontations of the day occurred in the show ring when Ch. Windsweep Ladysman met Ch. Torohill Trader at the Morris and Essex show of 1934. Judged by Harold Johnson (owner of the Midbrook Kennels of Long Island), Ladysman was in for Specials while Trader was making his debut being ably handled by Bain Cobb, manager for Leonard Buck's Blackstone Kennel. Trader came up from the classes to Best of Winners and met Ladysman for Best of Breed. Mr. Johnson decided in favor of Trader and launched his record-breaking career. It was his great movement that was in large measure responsible for his appeal and popularity. A sluggish dog and a lazy dog on the bench; the minute Bain Cobb put him down in the show ring he electrified the spectators with his unsurpassed showmanship. Up to that time, there had been no dog matching Trader in flash, in his instinct for a flawless performance, and his ability to overcome competition and win the plaudits of the crowd.

As a sire, this great Black dog gave immeasurable help to the breed. He was behind the pedigree of the immortal Ch. Stockdale Town Talk as well as many other great ones. He carried on the long, graceful necks we see today, stamped his progeny with clean shoulders, and straight short backs. He put the Cocker "up" on the leg and was responsible for the gently sloping topline, withers to tail, so necessary to the perfect outline and type.

Following Torohill Trader, My Own Brucie was the next in the cycle of famous Cockers. Mellenthin seldom introduced a dog to the public until it was three or four years old. The Poughkeepsie genius did not believe a Cocker was at his show peak until thoroughly matured. Brucie, a "farmed out" product, did not do well at first. Mrs. Constance Wall, when judging one of the New Jersey shows, put Brucie down in his class. Later, Ch. Blackstone Reflector defeated Brucie several times. But in Chicago under Harry McTavey, Brucie turned the tables and from then on could not be stopped. Taking nothing away from Brucie's greatness, he was not the showman Trader was. Brucie had his off moments when even Mellenthin could not get him to move with the necessary verve and

Ch. Try-Cob's Candidate

gaiety. When so disposed, My Own Brucie was a perfect show dog. He stands out as probably the most publicized Cocker Spaniel of all time. Winning Best in Show at Westminster, in 1940, was of tremendous value to the breed. No Cocker had done this since 1921, and then go back the next year and repeat the sensational win made the public truly Cocker Spaniel conscious. My Own Brucie did more to create interest in the Cocker than any other dog.

An understanding of his great popularity can be gained from the fact that when he passed away in the early 40's, the *New York Evening Sun* published his obituary on its front page, crowding out the war news to make room for it.

With the passing of Herman Mellenthin and My Own Brucie, a chapter in the book of American Cocker Spaniels was closed. Another was to begin with R. Kenneth Cobb and a dog called Ch. Try-Cob's Candidate. Ken Cobb (a brother of Bain Cobb and Trader's handler in all his triumphs), entered the dog world as manager of the Holmeric Kennels of New York. One of the most noted dogs from that kennel which Cobb put through to his championship was Ch. Mr. Holmeric, the sire of Ch. Holmeric of Brookville, himself the sire of 19 champions.

With the closing of Holmeric Kennel, Cobb opened his own place at Huntington, Long Island, New York, where, with Candidate, he was soon to top all other Cocker breeders both from the point of winning and stud services. Candidate, one of the happiest and most fearless Cockers, established his own bloodlines on the Foreglow foundation and an English Cocker outcross. From this cross came Ch. Nonquitt Nola's Candidate, Ch. Try-Cob's Favorite Girl, and a host of other well-known

Ch. Holmeric of Brookville

champions. All this stemming from Ch. Holmeric of Brookville through Try-Cob's Suzie Q (one of the finest producing bitches in the country).

On the west coast, C.B. Van Meter had established the Stockdale Kennel at Van Nuys, California. From this kennel came many sensational Cockers, among them the noted Ch. Stockdale Town Talk. Town Talk was brought east in 1944, to the Westminster show, defeated Ch. Nonquitt Nola's Candidate for Best of Variety and then won the Sporting group. Town Talk went on to sire 80 champions.

Ch. Stockdale Town Talk

Other breeders of this era who made important names for their kennels and finished many champions were the Pinfair Kennels of Mrs. H. Terrel Van Ingen, Greenwich, Connecticut; Mr. and Mrs. Hagood Bostick, Columbia, South Carolina; the Log O'Cheer Kennels of Birmingham, Alabama; the Claythorne Kennels of Mr. and Mrs. Joseph Crabbe, Cleveland, Ohio; the Easdale Cocker Kennels, owned by George Wuchter, Akron, Ohio; the Windridge Kennel owned by Arline Swalwell, Everett, Washington; the Bob-Bets Kennel of Robert Gusman, Atlanta, Georgia; the kennels of Andrew Hodges, on Long Island, New York; the Sugartown Kennels of Dr. and Mrs. Lewis Hart Marks, Paoli, Pennsylvania; and the Maplecliff Kennels of the Dautel's at Chesterland, Ohio. All were built on the foundation of Blackstone Chief and his son Foreglow.

CHAPTER 4

The Golden Era
Resurgence of the Breed

During its heyday, from 1936 until 1952, the Cocker Spaniel captured the top spot in AKC registrations and held it firmly for 16 years. The breed went into a decline after that time and actually, after a period of years, slipped out of the top ten in AKC registrations.

As happens to almost all overly popular breeds, too many breeders (who bred solely for profit) lept in to bring about a deterioration of the breed. Puppy mills spawned "Cockers" by the thousands. These animals, who were shipped far and wide from their homes in the mid-west, along with the other fast-buck opportunists who bred only to cash in on the breed's popularity, brought the quality and disposition of the merry Cocker to a sorry state.

Coupled with the decline in quality, the pet-buying public saw that the breed was almost rent asunder by the problem of "Juvenile Cataracts." Many famous dogs were accused of perpetuating the dreaded fault and a witch hunt ensued. Thank goodness for cooler and saner heads. Mari Doty and her *American Cocker Review* (ACR) magazine began to air the issue and supported a campaign to research the problem.

William L. Yakely, D.V.M. at Washington State University began a multi-year study into the problem. His research was supported, in part, by contributions encouraged by the *ACR*.

The American Spaniel Club became alarmed by the problem and began an annual Health Registry, in early 1976, to include cataract-free dogs and also dogs tested for Factor 10 (a blood clotting problem). Progressive retinal atrophy (PRA) and hip dysplasia (HD) were also included. The club formed the Hereditary and Congenital Defects Committee to deal with these problems and to publish the Registry. The compendium has been published yearly since then. While not fully eradicated, the cataract problem seems well under control today.

The drop from the lofty Number One position also brought new and very capable people onto the scene. Ruth and Art Benhoff come to mind immediately. Ruth was voted the Breeder of the Century by the ASC at their 100th anniversary show in 1981. Having bred over 100 champions and been an adviser to nearly everyone, it was an honor richly deserved. She, along with Herman Mellenthin and C.B. Van Meter, will stand on a pedestal in the Cocker Hall of Fame.

Listing everyone who made a major contribution to the breed since the close of World War II would fill two books. However, I will give my own biased views. Having lived and judged in all parts of the country, I have had the privilege of knowing many of the stalwarts of our time.

Tom O'Neal, a two-term president of the ASC, with his "Dreamridge" prefix dominated the Parti-Color scene for well over 20 years. This would not have been possible without his teaming-up with one of the most successful of handlers, Ron Fabis. Ch. Dreamridge Dominoe, the sire of over 100 champions and Ch. Dreamridge Dinner Date headline this kennel's achievements.

Another daring duo, that preceded O'Neal and Fabis, was the one-two punch of Bea Wegusen and Norman Austin. Bea with her famous Parti-Color Honey Creek Kennel, together with Norman, one of the foremost handlers of that day, made Cocker history with their multiple champion litters.

A major success story is that of Mari and Norm Doty and their string of Nor-Mar Champions and her wonderful work with the *American Cocker Review.*

Bud and Ida Hamsher put their imprint on the breed with their Shiloh Dell Cockers in Ohio.

The Kraeuchi's of St. Louis, Missouri produced top winners like clockwork at their famous Silver Maple Kennel. Ruth was also an author of note, having penned two books on the Cocker.

Byron and Cameron Covey, and their outstanding dogs in all colors, were preeminent on the west coast under the Camby prefix. Their son, Bob, is one of the top handlers of the breed today.

Carl and Rosalie Anderson, two of our popular judges today, were quite successful under the Carro prefix. Carl was a top-notch handler and their son, Gregg, has followed in his dad's footsteps.

Kudos to Jean Petersen, a past vice president of the Spaniel Club, and her history-making Ch. Rinky Dink's Sir Lancelot, a Black/Tan dog and a top-producing Cocker. I vividly remember judging the 1977 ASC futurity and thinking how alike my Black class winners were, and later finding out that three of the four were sired by Lance.

Edna Anselmi has long been a dominant force in the breed with her Windy Hill Kennels. Her dogs, headlined by Ch. Windy Hill's 'Tis Demi's Demon (sire of 83 champions), are among the top-producing dogs and bitches in the breed. Edna is also a judge.

Jim and Beth Hall in Washington State, whose astute breeding created the bloodlines that produced Ch. Scioto Bluff's Sinbad (sire of 118 champions) who, in turn, sired Dominoe, are to be highlighted for their leadership in furthering the cross between buffs and partis.

During the dark days between 1952 and 1977 only one Cocker, Ch. Carmor's Rise and Shine, won Best in Show at Westminster. He was handled by one of the most noted handlers of our time, Ted Young Jr. Ted's accomplishments are legendary. He was, for many years, the president of the Professional Handlers Association.

A model of a small kennel that made it in a big way is the Camelot Kennels of Lou and Amy Weiss of Sacramento, California. Their Black bitches are a sight to behold. Anita Roberts of Novato, California is another small-scale breeder who has done very well. Anita has also joined the ranks of famous judges of our day.

Harriet Kamps in Maryland, with her "Kamps" prefix, produced Kaptain Kool and Kojak along with other great ones. I have always admired the way she sets up a dog.

Laura and Kap Henson and their Kaplar prefix are in the forefront of breeders today. They have been the most consistent breeders of high-quality Cockers in the last 20 years. In fact, I have learned they were the top-producing kennel in England for 1985 and 1986 as well. Laura is also a consistent winner handling in the ring.

Dee Jurkiewicz, of Palm Hill fame, has made many sit up and take notice. Dee's bitches are behind some of the top-winning dogs of the day.

Hugh and Marilyn Spacht rode high with their top winning ASCOB dogs. These boys were producers as well as winners.

Lloyd Alton and Bill Gurodner for their special parti-colors—Bill's articles and Lloyd the "famous" announcer at all the ASC shows who occasionally lets me sit up on the platform with him.

Along about 1977, the fortunes of the breed took a turn for the better and the breed began a slow but accelerating climb back into the "top ten" in registrations. The year began auspiciously when a record futurity entry of 208 puppies were entered at the ASC show. It began to be evident that the hard work of the ASC and the *ACR* magazine had begun to pay off. By then the puppy mills had gone on to other breeds and the fast-buck operators were avoiding Cockers.

During the hiatus from the top rungs, the breed went through a number of metamorphoses. In the 1950's, the standard was changed to limit the height to 15 ½ inches. A further standard change better specified the range of allowable markings on the black and tan. Still another change in the 70's more exactly specified the height/length ratio. And finally, in the early 80's, the black and tan was included with the Black variety; the liver and tan was recognized officially and placed in the ASCOB (**A**ny **S**olid **C**olor **O**ther **T**han **B**lack) variety; and tri-color markings were specified more clearly.

The Spaniel Club, with great support from the membership, developed a summer national show. Officially known as the National Cocker Spaniel Specialty, this rotating specialty is for American Cockers only. This premier event is now a fixture. How did we ever do without it?

The breed has prospered. New clubs and new fanciers are everywhere and entries at the shows are excellent. An interesting observation of what happened to our breed during 1952-1977 is that while registrations dropped, show entries and top-winning Cockers did not show any real decline.

CHAPTER 5

Form Follows Function

That form follows function is very important for you, as a breeder, to know. In many ways that is a way to tell the differences in many breeds. A Cocker Spaniel with its long neck—allowing the nose to be close to the ground so its long ears can help waft the scent of game is a good example. The galloping, hunting hound, because of its function, has a unique physical form (flexible spine, arched loin with somewhat sloping croup and low tailset and flat ribs) follows the function which is the speed to run down game and/or kill or hold for the hunter. Or the Dachshund, whose function is to go to ground after game (up to and including the dangerous badger), has the form to perform such work—long, low body, heavy bone and digging feet, and a long, powerful head and jaw.

If you have ever designed anything with functional parts, you know that structural design implies more than bare bones of anatomy. A good design takes into account all factors that will help the structure serve its purpose. Similarly, the structural design of a dog must provide for all the needs of its owner.

In keeping with the principles of good architectural design, body and head structure must take into account the specific properties the animal uses in his work. These materials must be able to withstand the stresses implicit in the design. Therefore, no breeder of a dog designed to herd flocks would think of placing a thin unprotected skin where a tough layer of subcutaneous muscle and bristly coat should go. Here again, the inter-relationship of structure and function is obvious—the two go together. One of the most important things in designing and working with any breed is to always keep in mind the inseparability of structure and function. That is, the form of the animal must be designed for the function for which it has been originally bred. Often breeders tamper with nature's design and produce dogs that have an overly short topline.

Mother Nature, seeing breeders tamper with the natural design of things, has pitched in to help solve the problem. She has helped to create a dog which could move correctly within the standard's measurements. She has done this by rotating the pelvis and croup (thus throwing the angle of the rear quarters further back and allowing for more time for the rear leg swing so the front has time to get out of the way).

What are the consequences of this engineering change? First, logically enough, with the changed angle of the croup, the Cocker now has a terrier tail. How some purists howl about this; not aware that they themselves caused the problem by invoking an improper standard change. The second consequence of the croup angle change is that there are fewer moving dogs who display a sloping topline. A level topline is what the croup change will produce.

The function for which dogs were originally bred is not the function for which they are utilized today. Most Cockers are kept in a house or apartment as the family pet and seldom have the opportunity to demonstrate their specific skills.

To go along with function we have established breed types. That is a physical form which allows the dog to perform its function and around which we can weave an artistic word description. The definition of breed is type. The division of animals into groups of their species, according to differences in physical type, is the basis of breeds. A definite recognizable type must be common to all members of the group. For, without BREED type there is no breed. A BREED is the highest form of a species, that over a number of generations of controlled breeding, has developed definite physical characteristics that, taken together, are the consistent type of that species.

Organic Engineering

You can get a better understanding of the functional aspects of a breed of dog if you think of them in terms of engineering. Consider, for example, the role of the early breeders in England. They had two kinds of jobs. First, they tried to design a useful product: a dog who could go after upland birds, stay close to the hunter, have a good nose, be steady and have the ability to go all day long in the field. Originally these hunting dogs had to put food on the table, only later were they hunted for sport. Then these early breeders had to find a way to manufacture these products. In bringing a new product into being, an engineer first lays out a method of operation. He might even design and build a new tool just for making this one product. With the breeder, he might bring in another breed and cross it and re-cross it and introduce others until he got the correct mixture. The breeder might have to go through dozens of developmental stages before turning out a satisfactory replica of the designed product. But no matter how many steps you must take, a good product engineer (breeder) never departs from the intent of the basic design. He recognizes that the design has a special purpose which his efforts must serve. The farmer in England, who had to protect his livestock and fowl against the incursion of foxes who holed up in dens in rocky lairs, invented a sturdy little dog to take care of that problem. This dog had to get along with the pack of hounds who were to be used to run the fox to ground. Added to the design was the necessity of having a skull and rib cage that were flat enough to allow him to squeeze into any crevice the fox could. Finally, to have punishing jaws to dispatch the fox and haul him out. This little dog was called the Lakeland Terrier. He is about the same size as the Cocker but certainly built for an expressly different function.

But whether we are talking about a dog breeder or an engineer, they both design their products or devise techniques to make use of certain basic designs. For example, an engineer must use only those geometrical figures that would yield desired structural strength. He must also use shapes that will conserve on materials and yet provide for the greatest efficiency. Furthermore, he must also concern himself with simplicity of design. Therefore, whenever possible he must construct simple machines (levers, pulleys, and inclined planes) rather than intricate combinations of these machines.

Obviously, a dog—or any living organism—is its own engineer. Throughout its life, it constantly refers to a basic design and manufactures the product it needs. In so doing, it makes use of the same principles of design that men use in building machines and other conveniences. The dog also makes use of the same mechanical principles that underline the operation of man-made devices. Consider, for example, the transmission of force. When an animal moves its movable parts, it transmits force in much the same way that machines do. In so doing, the animal uses its built-in, simple machines. You can see this quite clearly in locomotor structures and that is why judging the gait of a dog in terms of its ability to perform its function is so very important in the overall approach to judging dogs.

Movement

For many years vast majority of dog people, and even physiologists, believed that animals running at higher speeds would exact a higher "cost" in terms of energy burned—it didn't turn out that way! Recent studies have shown that animals use up energy at a uniform, predictable rate as the speed of movement increases.

As if that shattering piece of information wasn't enough—they found out that for any given animal, the amount of energy expended in getting from point A to point B was the same regardless of how fast the trip was taken. A Cheetah running 100 yards at a top speed of 60 mph, uses the same amount of energy as it would *walking* the same distance. The running is more exhausting because the calories are used up more quickly.

Size, however, does make a difference. Small dogs require much more energy per unit of weight to run at top speed than a Great Dane would. Small dogs appear to have higher "idling" speeds. The cost of maintaining muscular tension and of stretching and shortening the muscles are higher in small animals.

These same series of studies suggest that as much as 77 percent of the energy used in walking comes, not from the operation of the muscles themselves, but from a continual interplay between gravity and kinetic energy. From an engineering standpoint it seems that the body tends to rotate about a center of mass, somewhat like an egg rolling end on end or the swing of an inverted pendulum. The 30 percent of effort supplied by the muscles is imparted through the limbs to the ground to keep the animal's center of mass moving forward.

At faster speeds, four-footed animals appear to be capable of calling into use a work-saving scheme that relies upon the elastic storage of energy in muscles and tendons. Some are better at it than others. Some are capable of storing more energy per stride than others.

During running or trotting the built-in springs for propulsion are the muscles and tendons of the limbs. When the animal has need to move even faster, he has the ability to use an even bigger spring. As the dog shifts from the fast trot to a gallop they tend to use their bodies as a large spring to store more energy. They do not change the frequency of their strides, rather they increase the length of them.

Simple Bio-Machines

Let us now consider how the dog compares with man-made machines. The dog can be compared to combinations of simple machines and other mechanical systems you might find in any factory. A few familiar examples will quickly clarify this analogy. The dog's legs for example. You could diagram them as levers. The appendages of all animals, in fact, serve as levers. If laid out side by side, they would present a rather special array of "machines." As we have certainly seen dogs—from the Chihuahua to the Great Dane—present a wide variety of angles and levers.

Of course you would expect this, for their owners have widely different ways of life. Modifications in such bio-levers reflect the animal's way of life. So you would expect the Saluki's leg to be the kind of lever that gives the advantage of speed and distance. By the same token, you would expect the design of the front legs of the Basset, "a burrowing animal," to provide for the multiplication of force, rather than the advantage of distance or speed.

Another simple machine that is easy to detect in nature is the pulley. You will find the living counterpart of the pulley wherever you find a muscle-tendon joint apparatus. Whenever a tendon moves over a joint, it behaves like a pulley. Such mechanisms enable the dog to change the direction of force. A notable example of an application of the pulley principle is the action of the tendons and muscles in the dog's neck. When the handler "strings the dog up" on a tight lead, the ability of the dog to use that pulley correctly is gone. What you have looks like a spastic alligator moving.

Inclined planes are prevalent in all living things, but their presence is not always obvious. They frequently appear as wedges, which are made up of two inclined planes arranged back-to-back. The incisors of the dog, for example, are wedges. The cutting action of these teeth is an application of the wedge principle in nature. The terrier-type of mouth is vastly different from that of the sporting dog. The sporting dog mouth is designed to hold a bird gently without crushing it. Therefore, its construction does not allow for great force to be generated. In contrast, the terrier jaws are punishing and can generate enough force to kill game.

Another illustration is when a standard calls for a sloping topline in movement. The sloping plane from withers to tail is designed to harness the thrust or drive from the rear quarters and move the dog along a straight line with power.

Hydraulics and Life

Any person who has tried to dam up a creek, or in some other way tried to manage moving water, has had experience with hydraulics. It involves the application of energy to practical uses. Frequently, therefore, hydraulics deals with the transfer of mechanical energy of moving fluids to the powering of machinery. It also deals with the use of pressure created by fluids (hydraulic pressure). All this, of course, finds an application in biology, wherein fluid is of paramount importance. Applications of hydraulic pressure are evident in dogs. Certainly the pumping action of the heart (as being responsible for the movement of blood through the circulatory system) is an appropriate example. A standard asking for a deep chest and the front wide enough for adequate heart and lung space is telling us we need room for a pump big enough to keep the dog going under pressure all day long. This pump exerts pressure, directly or indirectly, on all body fluids. As you know, when the heart is in need of repair or is worn out, the blood pressure of the animal varies abnormally. When this happens, the animal finds it hard to maintain a proper fluid balance of its tissues and organs. The final result is interference with the movement of the materials of life. Death can occur if the equipment designed to maintain hydraulic pressure fails in its function. As you may recall from your school studies of anatomy, it takes more than the pumping of the heart to maintain normal fluid pressure in an animal. The condition of the arteries and the veins is equally important. If these circulatory structures do not have the proper strength or elasticity, this condition could cause abnormal variation in the hydraulic pressure of the body. The arteries and veins are fluid conduits. Therefore, they must have a structural design that will enable them to withstand and adjust to sudden changes in hydraulic pressure.

From your studies, you may recall how effectively the design met the need. The walls of the arteries are designed to have heavier muscular construction than the veins. That's because the blood being pumped under great pressure from the heart goes out through the arteries and returns under less pressure through the veins. Thus, the arteries can withstand greater pressure than the veins can tolerate. The arteries tend to be more elastic than the veins so they can react more quickly to changes in pressure and so regulate the movement of fluid to compensate for the change in the situation.

Organic Architecture (Type)

The shape of a building usually reflects its function. The design of its various parts (roof, doors, ventilators) also relates to special functions. So it is with the shape of the dog. In a large dog, the design often calls for a shape that will provide the necessary strength, compactness and capability to perform certain functions. For example, dogs such as the Malamute were used to haul heavy loads. They were designed with a shoulder construction and balanced size that would enable them to perform this function. On the other hand, for example, a long and slender shape characterizes the coursing type of dog (Afghan, Greyhound, Borzoi and Saluki). This shape facilitates the faster movement of energy from place to place. The Cocker, on the other hand, is designed with a balanced shape to be neither a hauler or speed demon, but to go at a moderate pace for a sustained period of time.

In all cases we need to consider how we recognize the shape we are dealing with. First we must consider outline. Outline encompasses every aspect of the individual animal, making it immediately clear as to what breed or species it belongs.

Structure, Shape and Symmetry

As we have noted, overall body shape has a definite relationship to a dog's way of life. It relates, for example, to the use of energy. It also has to do with the animal's ability to relate to its environment and to perform the function for which it was originally bred. As you continue to study dogs, you will see more and more how the shape of things facilitates their function. Take the opportunity to see how the smooth functioning of an animal or of its parts, relates to its function.

A major identifying characteristic of a breed is its head. The head and expression is the very essence of a dog. Without proper breed type, an individual is just a dog, not a Cocker, a Springer or even a Great Dane.

Balance is also very important. No part should be longer, shorter, larger or smaller than is compatible with the whole. Everything must fit together to form a pleasing picture of "rightness."

Most breed standards call for a short back. Rightly so, for this is where the strength is. However, a short back is not synonymous with a short dog. The back is actually that small portion of the topline which lies between the base of the withers and the loin. A dog with a long sloping shoulder and a long hip may give the impression of a longer dog. A dog which gives the impression of being taller than it is long, is a dog badly out of balance. This dog is quite likely to have such a short croup that it appears to have none at all. A short steep croup will straighten the leg bones and leads to a highly ineffective and inefficient rear movement. A dog properly angulated at one end, but not on the other, is in even worse balance.

The too-upright shoulder is probably the worst imbalance of all because it affects every other part of the body. It puts great stress on a moving dog, making it pound its front feet into the ground, or crab sidewise to avoid interference with its hind feet.

As you look at your dog in the yard at home, in the show ring or out in the field working birds, look for the features of its design that might account for its survival and popularity. Look for the relationship of structural design to vital functions. Ask yourself. "How is this shape most suitable for the function of this structure?" "How is the body shape of this animal related to the environment in which it has to live?" In searching for answers, go beyond the obvious facts and look for subtle relationships. Look for special problems. For example, in reading many of the breed magazines today, we find breeders bewailing the promiscuous breedings and the terrible things that have happened to their breed. They often point out their breed is no longer able to perform its primary function because of straight shoulders, over-angulated rears or too much coat. Their claim is the breed is no longer functional. FORM NO LONGER FOLLOWS FUNCTION!...What are the breeders of today going to do about it?

CHAPTER 6

General Appearance—The Standard of the Breed

The Cocker Spaniel is the smallest member of the Sporting Group. He has a sturdy, compact body and a cleanly chiseled and refined head, with the overall dog in complete balance and of ideal size. He stands well up at the shoulder on straight forelegs with a topline sloping slightly toward strong, moderately bent, muscular quarters. He is a dog capable of considerable speed, combined with great endurance. Above all, he must be free and merry, sound, well balanced throughout and in action show a keen inclination to work. A dog well balanced in all parts is more desirable than a dog with strongly contrasting good points and faults.

Size, Proportion, Substance

Size

The ideal height at the withers for an adult dog is 15 inches and for an adult bitch, 14 inches. Height may vary one-half inch above or below this ideal. A dog whose height exceeds 15-½ inches or a bitch whose height exceeds 14-½ inches shall be disqualified. An adult dog whose height is less than 14-½ inches and an adult bitch whose height is less than 13-½ inches shall be penalized. Height is determined by a line perpendicular to the ground from the top of the shoulder blades, the dog standing naturally with its forelegs and lower hind legs parallel to the line of measurement.

Proportion

The measurement from the breast bone to back of thigh is slightly longer than the measurement from the highest point of withers to the ground. The body must be of sufficient length to permit a straight and free stride; the dog never appears long and low.

Head

To attain a well proportioned head, which must be in balance with the rest of the dog, it embodies the following:

Expression   The expression is intelligent, alert, soft and appealing.

Eyes   Eyeballs are round and full and look directly forward. The shape of the eye rims gives a slightly almond shaped appearance; the eye is not weak or goggled. The color of the iris is dark brown and in general the darker the better.

Ears   Lobular, long, of fine leather, well feathered, and placed no higher than a line to the lower part of the eye.

Skull   Rounded but not exaggerated with no tendency toward flatness; the eyebrows are clearly defined with a pronounced stop. The bony structure beneath the eyes is well chiseled with no prominence in the cheeks. The muzzle is broad and deep, with square even jaws. To be in correct balance, the distance from the stop to the tip of the nose is one half the distance from the stop up over the crown to the base of the skull.

Nose   Of sufficient size to balance the muzzle and foreface, with well developed nostrils typical of a sporting dog. It is black in color in the blacks, black and tans, and black and whites; in other colors it may be brown, liver or black, the darker the better. The color of nose harmonizes with the color of the eye rim.

Lips   The upper lip is full and of sufficient depth to cover the lower jaw.

Teeth   Teeth strong and sound, not too small and meet in a scissors bite.

Neck, Topline, Body

Neck   The neck is sufficiently long to allow the nose to reach the ground easily, muscular and free from pendulous "throatiness." It rises strongly from the shoulders and arches slightly as it tapers to join the head.

Topline   Sloping slightly toward muscular quarters.

Body   The chest is deep, its lowest point no higher than the elbows, its front sufficiently wide for adequate heart and lung space, yet not so wide as to interfere with the straightforward movement of the forelegs. Ribs are deep and well sprung. Back is strong and sloping evenly and slightly downward from the shoulders to the set-on of the docked tail. The docked tail is set on and carried on a line with the topline of the back, or slightly higher; never straight up like a Terrier and never so low as to indicate timidity. When the dog is in motion the tail action is merry.

Forequarters

The shoulders are well laid back forming an angle with the upper arm of approximately 90 degrees which permits the dog to move his forelegs in an easy manner with forward reach. Shoulders are clean-cut and sloping without protrusion and so set that the upper points of the withers are at an angle which permits a wide spring of rib. When viewed from the side with the forelegs vertical, the elbow is directly below the highest point of the shoulder blade. Forelegs are parallel, straight, strongly boned and muscular and set close to the body well under the scapulae. The pasterns are short and strong. Dewclaws on forelegs may be removed. Feet compact, large, round and firm with horny pads; they turn neither in nor out.

Hindquarters

Hips are wide and quarters well rounded and muscular. When viewed from behind, the hind legs are parallel when in motion and at rest. The hind legs are strongly boned, and muscled with moderate angulation at the stifle and powerful, clearly defined thighs. The stifle is strong and there is no slippage of it in motion or when standing. The hocks are strong and well let down. Dewclaws on hind legs may be removed.

Coat

On the head, short and fine; on the body, medium length, with enough undercoating to give protection. The ears, chest, abdomen and legs are well feathered, but not so excessively as to hide the Cocker Spaniel's true lines and movement or affect his appearance and function as a moderately coated sporting dog. The texture is most important. The coat is silky, flat or slightly wavy and of a texture which permits easy care. Excessive coat or curly or cottony textured coat shall be severely penalized. Use of electric clippers on the back coat is not desirable. Trimming to enhance the dog's true lines should be done to appear as natural as possible.

Color and Markings

Black Variety	Solid color black to include black with tan points. The black should be jet; shadings of brown or liver in the coat are not desirable. A small amount of white on the chest and/or throat is allowed; white in any other location shall disqualify.
Any Solid Color Other than Black (ASCOB)	Any solid color other than black, ranging from lightest cream to darkest red, including brown and brown with tan points. The color shall be of a uniform shade, but lighter color of the feathering is permissible. A small amount of white on the chest and/or throat is allowed; white in any other location shall disqualify.
Parti-Color Variety	Two or more solid, well broken colors, one of which must be white; black and white, red and white (the red may range from lightest cream to darkest red), brown and white, and roans, to include any such color combination with tan points. It is preferable that the tan markings be

located in the same pattern as for the tan points in the Black and ASCOB varieties. Roans are classified as parti-colors and may be of any of the usual roaning patterns. Primary color which is ninety percent (90%) or more shall disqualify.

Tan Points The color of the tan may be from the lightest cream to the darkest red and is restricted to ten percent (10%) or less of the color of the specimen; tan markings in excess of that amount shall disqualify. In the case of tan points in the Black or ASCOB variety, the markings shall be located as follows:

1) A clear tan spot over each eye;

2) On the sides of the muzzle and on the cheeks;

3) On the underside of the ears;

4) On all feet and/or legs;

5) Under the tail;

6) On the chest, optional; presence or absence shall not be penalized.

Tan markings which are not readily visible or which amount only to traces, shall be penalized. Tan on the muzzle which extends upward, over and joins shall also be penalized. The absence of tan markings in the Black or ASCOB variety in any of the specified locations in any otherwise tan-pointed dog shall disqualify.

Gait

The Cocker Spaniel, though the smallest of the sporting dogs, possesses a typical sporting dog gait. Prerequisite to good movement is balance between the front and rear assemblies. He drives with strong, powerful rear quarters and is properly constructed in the shoulders and forelegs so that he can reach forward without constriction in a full stride to counterbalance the driving force from the rear. Above all, his gait is coordinated, smooth and effortless. The dog must cover ground with his action; excessive animation should not be mistaken for proper gait.

Temperament

Equable in temperament with no suggestion of timidity.

Disqualifications

Height	Males over 15-½ inches; females over 14-½ inches.
Color and Markings	The aforementioned colors are the only acceptable colors or combination of colors. Any other colors or combination of colors to disqualify.
Black Variety	White markings except on chest and throat.
ASCOB Variety	White markings except on chest and throat.
Parti-color Variety	Primary color ninety percent (90%) or more. Tan Points (1) Tan markings in excess of ten percent (10%); (2) Absence of tan markings in Black or ASCOB Variety in any of the specified locations in an otherwise tan pointed dog.

CHAPTER 7

They Come In Coats of Many Hues

Because of the great variety of colors allowable under the Cocker Spaniel standard, color genetics have always held a fascination for the breeder. No sooner is a breeding made than the breeder begins to wonder what colors the litter will contain. Unfortunately, many breed on a "hit or miss" basis and are completely surprised by the results.

Blacks

"A good dog is a good color" is a statement that is often quoted and one with which most breeders seem to agree.

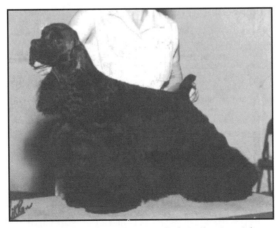

Ch. Bobuin's Sir Ashley—A Black Cocker Spaniel.

Certain physical traits can be associated or linked with certain colors. This is much less the case today because of the use of the dilute type breeding in all three varieties. This has caused a "homogenization" process of the varieties.

Fifty years ago the blacks were generally acknowledged as being superior to all other colors. Viewing a show from ringside, an impartial observer of the time would have been forced to concede that the blacks, and parti-colors were two separate breeds.

One of the major differences between the blacks and the Cockers of other colors was coat. Only a few of the black and tans carried good coat. A buff or parti-color with a heavy coat was rarely seen. Therefore, the most obvious physical trait associated with the blacks was coat.

There were also other superior traits with the blacks. Among these traits were flatter and heavier bone, better top line, shorter backs, smoother muscles (and different muscular placement), better chiseling, etc. This all pointed to the fact that a color linkage (a tendency of certain characteristics to appear together because the genes for those characteristics are located on the same chromosome) exists between the black color and desirable features of conformation.

This was proven time and again when black puppies born of parents that were other than black tended to be of "black type" while litter mates of other colors were not.

Many sparsely coated buffs and parti-colors were bred to blacks in the hope of attaining coat. However, in the resulting litters only the black offspring carried "black type" coats. This highlights a key factor in color breeding and one focused on throughout this chapter, namely with the infusion of the dilution gene, certain blacks can pass on "black type" characteristics to their recessive colored offspring.

With blacks, as with Cockers; of all colors, there are multiple genotypes (genotype is the sum of a dog's contribution to its offspring phenotype, on the other hand is surface color or other characteristics). The surface color does not tell the full story. It is necessary to do test matings or have pedigrees that are truly informative as to what the dogs in the preceding generations produced.

As breeders, most have long believed that there was a dominant black and a recessive black, and only one kind of liver; the same was thought to be true for the buff color. These assumptions are not entirely true. The following pages delve into the various color combinations that are possible

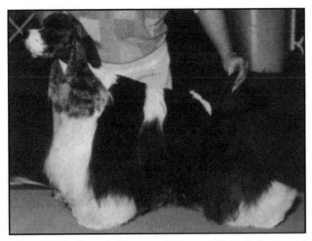

Ch. Paradise's Blue Rebel Rouser—A Blue and White Cocker Spaniel

within the breed. Certainly a wide variety of colors is possible, but not always accepted by the breeders. The sable and sable/white colors are an example. Many people bred them and some finished their championships, but their adherents were unable to muster the two-thirds vote necessary to allow them a place in the standard. Today we are seeing some breeders beginning to push a "bluish" color dog. Its fate remains to be seen. Figure 1 illustrates the nine levels of dominance in the breed. As you will note, there are four distinct types of blacks. The Class Number 2 black explains how the dilute blacks came about. The dilute black is, in reality, a buff dog who is black in all his characteristics—the same genotype but different phenotype—he lacks the ability to extend his black factor into his coat color.

There is no way to differentiate these four types of black just by appearance. Knowledge of specific pedigrees can point out differences in some cases but the true test comes in breeding.

All mating ratios given here are based on the laws of averages. The larger the litter, the better the chance of coming up with the specified ratios. The smaller the litter, the poorer the chance. However, should the smaller litter be repeated once or twice more, the breeder would then find the specified ratios would probably hold true. Today the vast majority of blacks are of the Class Number 2, Class Number 3, and Class Number 4 hybrids. Alas, the dominant black is seldom found, for breeders—in their desire to get a variety of colors—have not sought to perpetuate this characteristic. Naturally, when a dominant black is bred to any

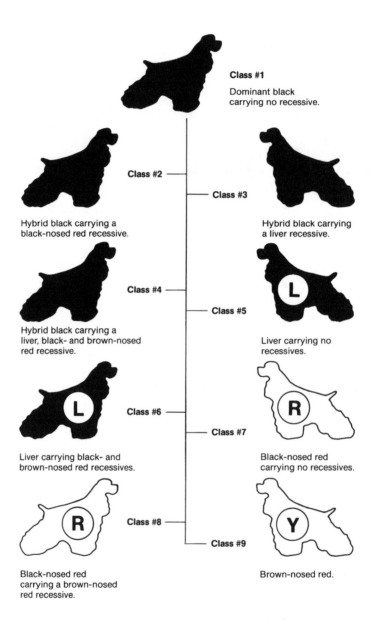

Class #1
Dominant black carrying no recessive.

Class #2

Class #3

Hybrid black carrying a black-nosed red recessive.

Hybrid black carrying a liver recessive.

Class #4

Class #5

Hybrid black carrying a liver, black- and brown-nosed red recessive.

Liver carrying no recessives.

Class #6

Class #7

Liver carrying black- and brown-nosed red recessives.

Black-nosed red carrying no recessives.

Class #8

Class #9

Black-nosed red carrying a brown-nosed red recessive.

Brown-nosed red.

Figure 1. Hierarchy of dominance in the solid-color Cocker Spaniel

other color only blacks will result. The section on mismarks spells this out further.

Buffs

Many years around the show ring have impressed me with the fact that there are more hues of buff coloration in Cockers than in any other breed. What makes "buff" so difficult to describe is the ambiguity of terminology—not only among breeders but also among geneticists. Such terms as "blond," "golden," "red," "dark buff," "silver," etc., all describe the buff-colored Cocker Spaniel. That same latitude is found in the black and tan Cocker whose description states the color may be from the lightest of cream to the darkest of red. Those same spectrum ranges are to be found in the buffs.

All of the variations in color describe phenotypes, but genotypically there are only three types of buffs. Two are described as "black-nosed reds" and one is called a "brown-nosed red."

The black-nosed reds can be differentiated only by test matings, for they produce quite differently from other buffs. One, the Class Number 7 black-nosed red, will not throw liver color regardless of the color of dog to which he is bred. This dog does not carry liver genes. He is further described under the section on chocolates (see Figures 2 and 3). This Class Number 7 black has been called a "dilute black." In fact, he is a black

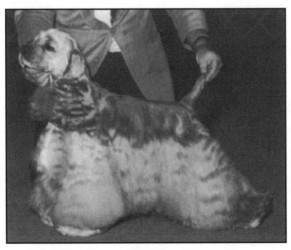

Ch. Tompark's Little Rock—A Buff Cocker Spaniel.

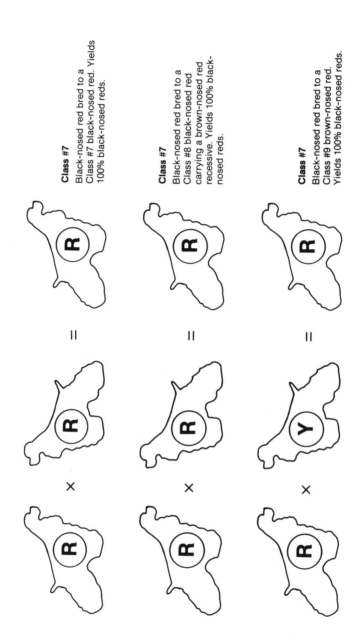

Class #7

Black-nosed red bred to a Class #7 black-nosed red. Yields 100% black-nosed reds.

Class #7

Black-nosed red bred to a Class #8 black-nosed red carrying a brown-nosed red recessive. Yields 100% black-nosed reds.

Class #7

Black-nosed red bred to a Class #9 brown-nosed red. Yields 100% black-nosed reds.

Figure 2. Buffs

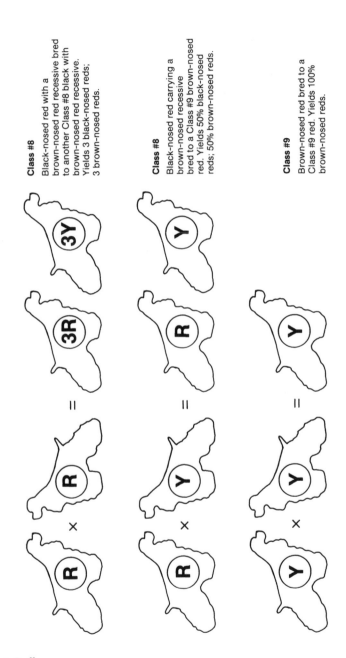

Class #8

Black-nosed red with a brown-nosed red recessive bred to another Class #8 black with brown-nosed red recessive. Yields 3 black-nosed reds; 3 brown-nosed reds.

Class #8

Black-nosed red carrying a brown-nosed recessive bred to a Class #9 brown-nosed red. Yields 50% black-nosed reds; 50% brown-nosed reds.

Class #9

Brown-nosed red bred to a Class #9 red. Yields 100% brown-nosed reds.

Figure 3. Buffs

who lacks the extension factor (the ability to extend black color through-out his coat). His nose, paws, and skin are usually blue/black or blue/black spotted. This dilute black has revolutionized the buff Cocker. Due to a genetic crossover (as explained in the next paragraph), it can pass black characteristics to all other colors. Before a "crossover" occurred, this was not possible. The Class Number 7 black-nosed red which has often been called a "black-nosed yellow, lacking the extension factor for black coat color," is genetically black in type and conformation but lacks the coat color. Now this is important! Because of the dilution factor, it is impossible to obtain dark reds and chocolates from breeding to a Class Number 7 black-nosed red.

Certain structural changes are commonly associated together. This is due to a phenomenon known as "linkage." Any body characteristic which is located in one pair of chromosomes—and in no other—will be inherited in accordance with Mendelian laws. Characteristics which have determiners (or genes located in different chromosomes) will be inde-pendent of one another in transmission. All possible combinations of them will occur just as various combinations of numbers appear when dice are cast…according to the laws of chance.

When two characteristics have genes located on the same chromo-some, they will stay together so long as the chromosome remains intact. Such characteristics are said to be "linked."

It is known that chromosomes are, at times, in close contact with their mates. At such a stage, breaks sometimes occur—usually at the same level in each chromosome of the pair. If the breaks are repaired in such a way as to cause the upper part of one chromosome to become attached to the lower part of its mate and vice versa, a regrouping of the genes occurs in the new cell. Such a phenomenon occurring in a germ cell is called "crossing over." This is illustrated in Figure 4.

Where it has been possible to study crossing over by statistical meth-ods, it has been found that the phenomenon occurs in definite percent-ages for the same characteristics. A single characteristic can have more than one gene, each of which may be located on a different chromosome. These act together in a cumulative manner. Research indicates that a crossover probably occurred in the buffs in the immediate ancestry of Ch. Maddie's Vagabond's Return. Literature of the day described dogs that are strikingly similar to the dilute blacks as we know them today.

The second type of black-nosed red is known as a Class Number 8 dog. While the Class Number 7 specimen appears to be yellow, lemon, or cream-colored, the Class Number 8 dog ranges the spectrum from light buff to dark red. The Class Number 8 dog can be used to produce both chocolates and dark reds.

Last, there is the brown-nosed red, or the Class Number 9 dog. Like the Class Number 7 buff, he is not really a buff at all. He is a chocolate lacking the ability to extend color throughout his coat. Instead of black markings on the skin and pads, this type of buff has chocolate markings.

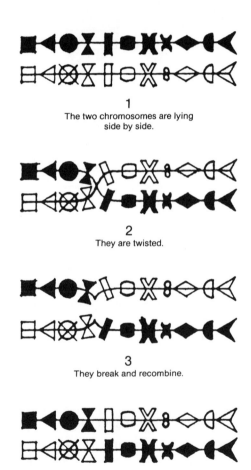

1
The two chromosomes are lying
side by side.

2
They are twisted.

3
They break and recombine.

Figure 4. Crossing over. Each geometric figure represents a gene. Allelomorphic genes occupy the same level on the two chromosomes. Identical shapes represent homozygotes; slightly different shapes represent heterozygotes. It will be noted that the linkage between the two adjacent heterozygotes below the break is unaffected, whereas the linkage between either of these and the heterozygote above the break is reversed. Where the characters on the two chromosomes were homozygous in the first place, the recombination has no effect on linkage.

Ch. Pineshadows Coco Cub-A Chocolate Cocker Spaniel

When bred to one type of chocolate, the Class Number 9 dog will produce only chocolates. When bred to a Class Number 6 chocolate, he will produce 50% chocolates. These three buffs—whose phenotypes look basically alike—are genetically different.

Chocolates

Liver or chocolate Cockers have been known in the breed since early times. Early breeders, unable to get dark eyes and noses and an acceptable coat, gave up on chocolates, for it was impossible to predict how they would reproduce.

Today, largely through the efforts of Arline Swalwell of Windridge Kennels, and the late Bill Ernst of Be Gay Kennels, handsome chocolates compete successfully within the ASCOB (Any Solid Color Other than Black) variety.

As in the buffs, there is more than one type of chocolate. Figure 5, shows that there is a Class Number 5 chocolate as well as a Class Number 6. The only way to determine *which* type chocolate is by test matings. The Class Number 5 dog, when bred to another Class Number 5 specimen, produces only chocolates. When the Number 5 dog is bred to a Class Number 6 type, again only chocolates are produced. However, when two Class Number 6 types are bred together, the predicted ratio is three chocolates to one brown-nosed red.

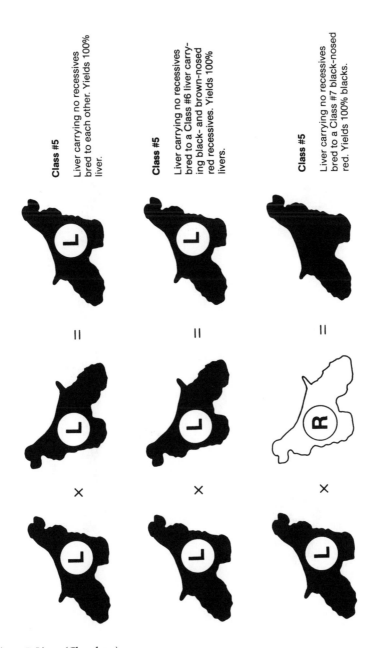

Class #5

Liver carrying no recessives bred to each other. Yields 100% liver.

Class #5

Liver carrying no recessives bred to a Class #6 liver carrying black- and brown-nosed red recessives. Yields 100% livers.

Class #5

Liver carrying no recessives bred to a Class #7 black-nosed red. Yields 100% blacks.

Figure 5. Livers (Chocolates)

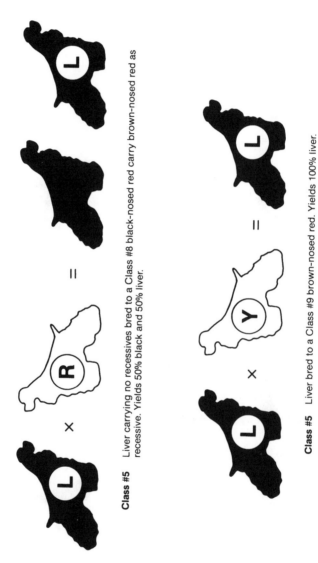

Class #5   Liver carrying no recessives bred to a Class #8 black-nosed red carry brown-nosed red as recessive. Yields 50% black and 50% liver.

Class #5   Liver bred to a Class #9 brown-nosed red. Yields 100% liver.

Figure 6. Livers (Chocolates), continued

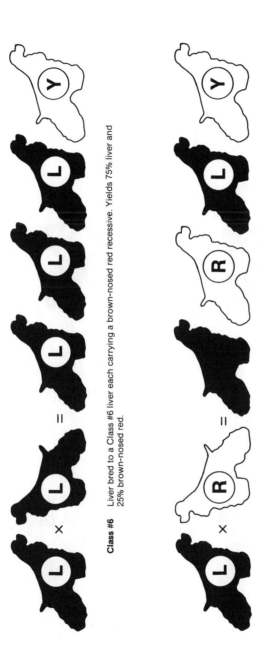

Class #6 Liver bred to a Class #6 liver each carrying a brown-nosed red recessive. Yields 75% liver and 25% brown-nosed red.

Class #6 Liver carrying a brown-nosed recessive bred to a Class #8 black-nosed red carrying a brown-nosed recessive. Yields 25% black, 25% black-nosed red, 25% liver, 25% brown-nosed red.

Figure 7. Livers (Chocolates), continued

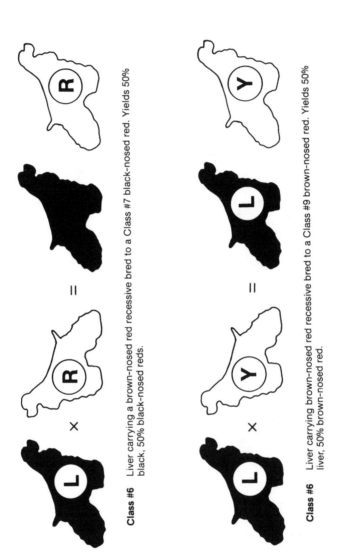

Figure 8. Livers (Chocolates), continued

When buff dogs are bred to each other, no matter what their geno-type, they cannot produce chocolates. Even the brown-nosed reds of Class Number 9 (which was described as a chocolate without the extension factor for chocolate color in its coat), when bred to another brown-nosed red, will produce only brown-nosed reds. It is evident, then, that in the hierarchy of dominance, solid black is first, followed by chocolate and then the buff/reds.

In the chocolates, hair grows as long, or nearly as long, as in the blacks but tends to have a softer, more wooly texture. From this, it can be concluded that wooly hair in chocolates is probably dominant. It is also important to know that in chocolates light noses and light eyes are dominant over dark.

In further discussions, this chapter will deal with hybrid-blacks, buff/reds, and chocolates. Figures 9-10 shows that a specimen cannot carry as a recessive, *the color of one above it in dominance.* Chocolate can be carried by a hybrid-black and can be reproduced at any time. The hybrid-black may also be carrying a recessive for buff/red, as well as black and tan and parti-color. A treasure chest this one!

The illustrations in Figures 11-19 give a good picture of what possible combinations can be realized in a solid-color breeding program. For more detailed information, I refer you to *Breeding Better Cocker Spaniels* by the author and published by Denlinger Publisher's, Ltd.

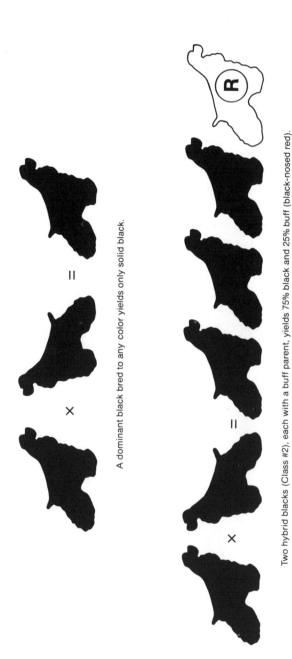

Figure 9. Blacks

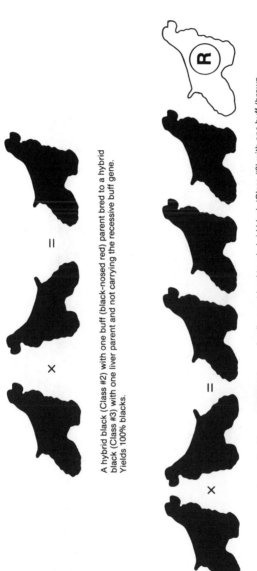

A hybrid black (Class #2) with one buff (black-nosed red) parent bred to a hybrid black (Class #3) with one liver parent and not carrying the recessive buff gene. Yields 100% blacks.

A hybrid black (Class #2) with one buff (black-nosed red) parent bred to a hybrid black (Class #3) with one buff (brown-nosed red) parent. Yields 75% black, 25% buff (black-nosed red).

Figure 10. Blacks, continued

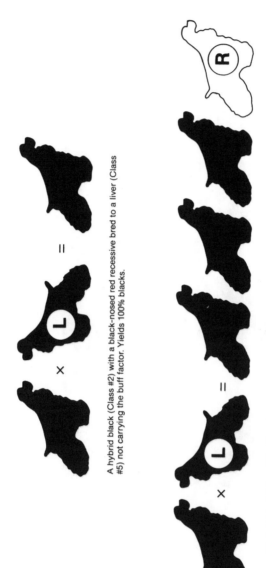

A hybrid black (Class #2) with a black-nosed red recessive bred to a liver (Class #5) not carrying the buff factor. Yields 100% blacks.

A hybrid black (Class #2) with a black-nosed red recessive bred to a liver (Class #6) carrying the buff factor (brown-nosed red). Yields 75% black and 25% buff (black-nosed red).

Figure 11. Blacks, continued

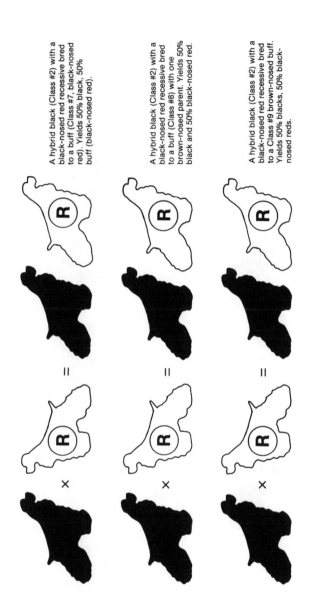

A hybrid black (Class #2) with a black-nosed red recessive bred to a buff (Class #7, black-nosed red). Yields 50% black, 50% buff (black-nosed red).

A hybrid black (Class #2) with a black-nosed red recessive bred to a buff (Class #8) with one brown-nosed parent. Yields 50% black and 50% black-nosed red.

A hybrid black (Class #2) with a black-nosed red recessive bred to a Class #9 brown-nosed buff. Yields 50% blacks, 50% black-nosed reds.

Figure 12. Blacks, continued

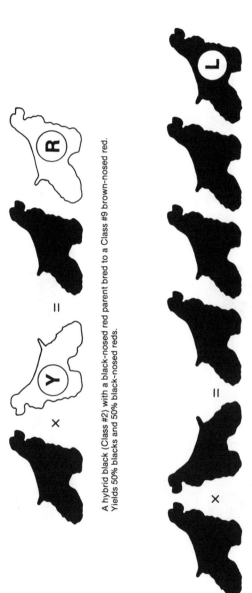

A hybrid black (Class #2) with a black-nosed red parent bred to a Class #9 brown-nosed red. Yields 50% blacks and 50% black-nosed reds.

A hybrid black (Class #3) having a liver recessive bred to another hybrid black with the same factors. Yields 75% blacks and 25% livers (chocolates).

Figure 13. Blacks, continued

A hybrid black (Class #3) having a liver recessive bred to a Class #4 black having liver and brown-nosed recessives. Yields 75% black and 25% liver (chocolate).

A hybrid black (Class #3) having a liver recessive bred to a Class #5 liver with no buff recessive. Yields 50% black and 50% liver (chocolate).

Figure 14. Blacks, continued

A hybrid black (Class #3) carrying a liver recessive bred to a Class #6 liver carrying a brown-nosed red recessive. Yields 50% black and 50% liver (chocolate).

A hybrid black (Class #3) carrying a liver recessive bred to a Class #7 black-nosed red not carrying the brown-nosed red factor. Yields 100% black.

Figure 15. Blacks, continued

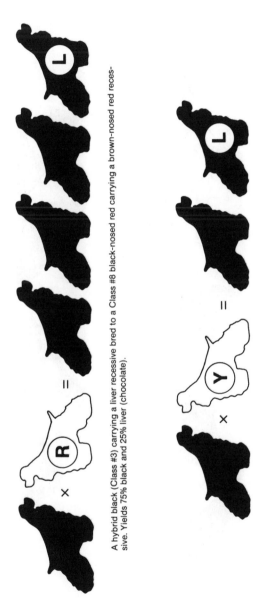

A hybrid black (Class #3) carrying a liver recessive bred to a Class #8 black-nosed red carrying a brown-nosed red recessive. Yields 75% black and 25% liver (chocolate).

A hybrid black (Class #3) carrying a liver recessive bred to a brown-nosed red Class #9. Yields 50% black and 50% liver (chocolate).

Figure 16. Blacks, continued

Two hybrid blacks (Class #4) carrying liver, black-nosed and brown-nosed reds bred to each other. Yields the perfect Mendelian ratio of 9:3:3:1.

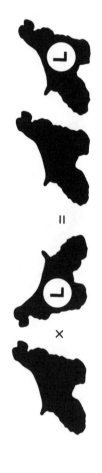

A hybrid black (Class #4) carrying recessives for liver, black-and brown-nosed reds bred to a Class #5 liver with no black-nosed red recessive. Yields 50% black and 50% liver (chocolate).

Figure 17. Blacks, continued

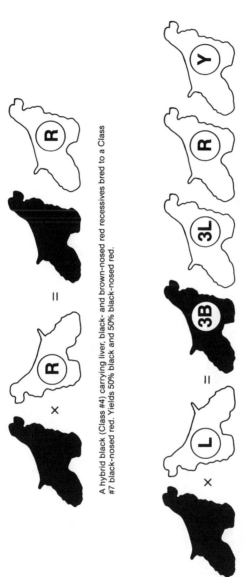

A hybrid black (Class #4) carrying liver, black- and brown-nosed red recessives bred to a Class #7 black-nosed red. Yields 50% black and 50% black-nosed red.

A hybrid black (Class #4) carrying recessives for liver, black- and brown-nosed reds bred to a Class #6 liver with black- and brown-nosed red recessives. Yields 3 blacks, 3 livers, 1 black-nosed red and 1 brown-nosed red.

Figure 18. Blacks, continued

A hybrid black (Class #4) carrying recessives for liver, black- and brown-nosed reds bred to a Class #8 black-nosed red carrying a brown-nosed red recessive. Yields 3 blacks, 3 black-nosed reds, 1 liver, 1 brown-nosed red.

A hybrid black (Class #4) carrying recessives for liver, black- and brown-nosed reds bred to Class #9 brown-nosed red. Yields 25% black, 25% black-nosed red, 25% liver and 25% brown-nosed red.

Figure 19. Blacks, continued

Ch. Hi-Boots Such Brass-A Black and Tan Cocker Spaniel

Bi-Colors

This coloration includes the black and tans, chocolate and tans, blue and tans, and red and tans. For most, the mention of the blue and tan and red and tans may seem puzzling for these colors are rarely seen. Well, rest assured, they are valid colors (see Figure 20 for full description).

In breeding bi-colors, one is dealing with a whole series of multiple recessives, something which is not present in any other color category in Cockers. These multiple recessives apply not only to coat color but also to characteristics that come to bi-colors through the colors of black, buff/red, chocolate, and white on some. The other colors in Cockers are a matter of single recessives or dominants in color inheritance. The sable color also uses multiple recessives to produce its pattern. In a bi-color, the solid color is not a dominant color but, rather is an "imperfect dominant."

The remarks and theories presented in the buff section apply equally to the bi-colors. Just because a dog is bi-color does not ensure that he will have the conformation or "type" of that color.

Bi-color is recessive to all solid colors. Solid colors can produce bi-color offspring only if both parents carry the recessive bi-color genes.

Since solid color is dominant, the recessive bi-color gene is denied expression when it is paired with a solid-color gene. The bi-color gene may be covered up by the solid-colored gene and handed down for many

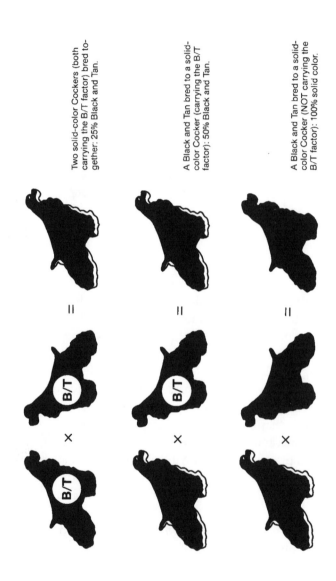

Figure 20. Black and Tans

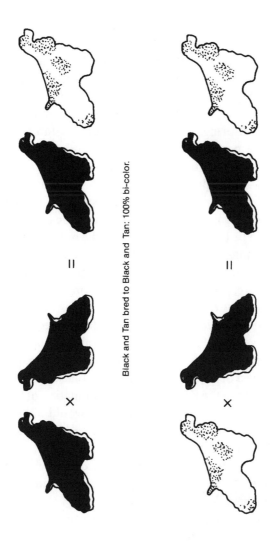

Black and Tan bred to Black and Tan: 100% bi-color.

Figure 21. Black and Tans, continued

generations. It is only when the bi-color gene becomes paired with another bi-colored gene that bi-color offspring result.

An example of this pattern being handed down for five generations without being seen was Ch. Bigg's Believe It Or Not, a black and tan who was Best in Show at the 1952 Annual Flushing Spaniel Specialty. His breeders, successful buff breeders, didn't dream the gene was there. Whether the bi-color offspring are black and tan, blue and tan, chocolate and tan, or buff/red and tan depends on what color the parents are and what colors they carry. Two buff/red parents cannot be expected to produce bi-color offspring. However, some of the buff/red puppies produced by these parents may be buff/red and tan with the contrast between the buff and tan being so slight as to make recognition of the pattern impossible. These puppies will, however, reproduce like bi-colors.

Matings of bi-color to bi-color can result in a small percentage of buff/red puppies. From the chocolate and tan, the expectation would be that they would be brown-nosed reds. All the buff/red puppies resulting from the breedings of bi-color parents are genotypically buff and tan. They look like solid buff/reds. The bi-color pattern is recessive to solid color, so therefore, two bi-color dogs cannot produce the dominant solid color. Buff and tan Cockers breed true insofar as the bi-color pattern is concerned. For example, if a buff/red and tan is bred to a black and tan who does not carry buff/red as a recessive, all the puppies will be black and tan in color. A black and tan not carrying buff/red as a recessive, bred to a solid buff/red or a buff/red carrying the black and tan factor, would produce all blacks in the first case and a combination of blacks and black and tans in the second instance. The same would hold true when the other bi-colors are bred this way. Thus, bi-color bred to bi-color produces 100 percent bi-color offspring.

Chocolate and tans mated to black-nosed reds which carry the pattern will produce black and tan puppies in true Mendelian ratio according to the genetic makeup of their parents.

Introduction of the dilution factor can cause the black to become blue, and chocolate to turn silver-fawn. This would explain the appearance of the blues that have been seen.

Bi-color has long been recognized as a *pattern* and this fact has been emphasized in the most recent standard change which now has a dog with tan markings in all three varieties. As a result, it now becomes important—in the breeding of bi-colors—to obtain a clear, easily recognizable pattern. Because the breeding of bi-colors is genetically a series of multiple factors, double matings are necessary to preserve the correct pattern. However, the constant breeding of bi-color to bi-color will tend to destroy the pattern. The sharpness and clarity will disappear and the pattern will become "fuzzy" and indistinct. Constant breeding of bi-color to bi-color may also result in less and less coat. If well-marked bi-colors are constantly bred together, the chances of getting overly marked dogs also increases. Breeding to solids with the bi-color factor can help to control this spread. Breeding to buff/reds with the bi-color factor can assist in increasing markings. A stage that falls in between is the brindling often seen on bi-colors.

Now is a good time to differentiate between brindling and pencilling. All bi-color dogs have some amount of pencilling. It looks like pencil marks on top of, but not intermixed with, the tan hairs. Brindling is different in that not all bi-colors are brindled. This is a condition in which black or chocolate hairs are intermixed throughout the tan pattern, resulting in a smudged, dirty, or gray look. Some say this is related to the sable pattern but I cannot vouch for that as fact.

Genetically, the clear copper-red color is dominant over all other colors in the bi-color pattern. Recessive to the clear copper color, yet dominant over the cream color, is brindling. Brindling is the first step in dilution from red. Recessive to both is the clear cream color.

Parti-Colors

The parti-color variety has made enormous strides over the past 40 years. At one time, the parti-colors seemed almost a separate breed, rather than a separate variety. What happened within recent memory to change this? First, Honey Creek Kennels revolutionized the parti-color by making them pretty and adding some coat. Then the same factors which changed the buff/reds caused a change in the partis. Better bone, toplines and coat became identified with partis as much as the other colors. The funny thing is that the early parti-colors coming from the dilute breedings were really not from the basic parti-color stock. Instead, the buff hairs were gradually diluted to a light lemon color which served as the "white" background upon which a red/tan color was superimposed. These dogs, when seen next to a white-background looked different than the normal parti-color.

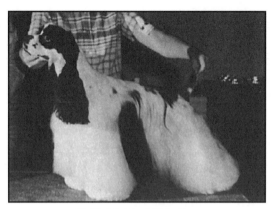

Ch. Yerly's Hot Off The Press
A Black and White Cocker Spaniel

When the genes which produce white spotting are combined with the genes which produce a black Cocker, a black and white is created. When the genes representing white spotting are combined with the genes which represent red, a red and white is created. The genes which produce white spotting are recessive to the genes which produce a completely solid-colored dog. Thus, white spotting is recessive to solid black, chocolate, buff/red and bi-color. As a result, when two dogs carrying the genes representing white spotting (or two parti-colors) are bred together, they can be expected to produce only parti-color offspring.

In parti-colors, ticking is dominant over plain white backgrounds but is also recessive to solid color. Roan, which is rare in the American Cocker but popular in the English Cocker, is usually superimposed upon ordinary ticking so that a mottled color results. Thus, roan is dominant over plain ticking, and ticking is dominant over pure white in the splashed areas.

In his book, *How to Breed Dogs*, Dr. Leon Whitney makes an interesting, general observation about black and white parti-colors. His observations led him to believe that black and white puppies usually have larger pigmented areas than do those of any other shade of red and white. This was subsequently borne out by Dr. C.C. Little at the Jackson Memorial Laboratory. Earlier investigations by Dr. Phillips (who did the pioneering work on color in Cockers), led him to conclude that red and whites usually have smaller areas of color than do black and whites in the same litter.

Ch. Kamps' Kaptain Kool
A Red and White Cocker Spaniel.

Therefore, the constant, promiscuous breeding of black and white to black and white results in more heavily-marked offspring in each succeeding generation. Continuous non-selective breeding of red and white to red and white usually shows a tendency for the white to increase in each succeeding generation. Today, it is evident that there are more and more puppies that show one-sided head markings and too much white on the body. In fact, there are ever increasing numbers of red and whites that barely have enough color to qualify as a parti-color.

In red and whites, both colors are recessive, while in black and whites, the black is dominant and the white recessive. Therefore, it is more difficult to breed consistently good black and whites. The dominant black in a black and white will have to be reduced to a state of "imperfect dominance" (as in the bi-colors) to allow consistently good black and whites to be bred. This seems to be happening. Carried to the extreme, black and whites can be produced rivaling their red and white brethren when it comes to lack of color. Parti-color breeders should be aware of losing the correct color pattern.

The percentage of black and white and/or red and white puppies expected in any given litter will depend upon the color of both the sire and dam and their backgrounds, and will follow the same inheritance pattern as the solid colors. For example, there are black and whites which, like dominant blacks, can produce nothing but black and whites when bred to a parti-color. These, when bred to a red and white, will

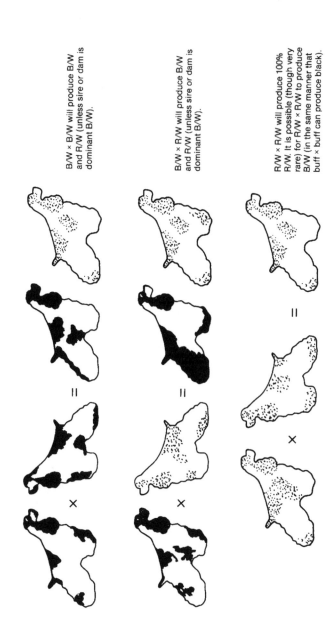

B/W × B/W will produce B/W and R/W (unless sire or dam is dominant B/W).

B/W × R/W will produce B/W and R/W (unless sire or dam is dominant B/W).

R/W × R/W will produce 100% R/W. It is possible (though very rare) for R/W × R/W to produce B/W (in the same manner that buff × buff can produce black).

Figure 22. Parti-Colors

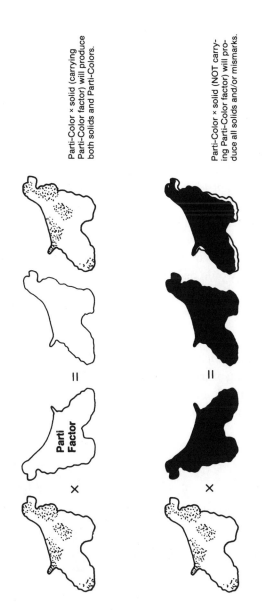

Figure 23. Parti-Colors, continued

produce 100% black and whites. In turn, however, the puppies will be hybrid and be able to produce both black and white and red and white. There are very few dominant black and white Cockers around, although they can, and do, exist.

Red and white when bred to red and white will usually produce only red and whites.

Applicable to the red and whites as well as to the buff/reds and bi-colors, are the different shades from Setter red to pale lemon. Variation in depth of shade within a continuous series of a single hereditary color variety is usually considered to be the result of so-called "modifying factors." These influence the degree of development or expression of the main genes which produce the color in question. Deep reds would be described as having "plus" modifiers which encourage the formation of more red pigment, while the lighter shades would be considered to be the result of "minus" modifiers which allow a lesser degree of red pigment to develop. Thinking of it in another way, hair follicles baked in the oven at 350° for 30 minutes would be lighter in color than ones that baked for an hour. Figures 22-23 illustrates the genetic combinations and results.

Tri-Colors

In the American Cocker Spaniel, a good deal of mystery has surrounded the breeding of tri-colors. True, tri-colors are not as common as their brethren the black and white and the red and white. However, the breeding of tri-colors should not be any more difficult than the breeding

Ch. Carronade Trigger—A Tri-Color Cocker Spaniel

of any other color. The major difficulties seem to be the ability to obtain desired markings (but lack of desirable comformation and type), or desired conformation and type (but lack of desirable markings). The purpose here will be to explain just what tri-colors are and to show how they can be obtained. Along these lines, perhaps some inferences can be drawn, showing how desired markings can be obtained along with desired conformation.

All of the remarks pertaining to the description of the bi-colored pattern and its variations apply equally to the tri-color pattern. Tri-color obviously means "three color," and, in dogs, one of these colors is always white. The other colors may be any one of the color combinations found in bi-color dogs, such as black and tan, chocolate and tan, blue and tan, or red and tan.

The foundation of the tri-color pattern is the bi-color pattern, the only difference being that tri-colors have inherited an independent set of genes which are capable of covering up a part of the bi-color pattern with white.

The amount of white found on tri-color dogs may vary from a great deal to very little. In Cockers, the genes for white spotting cover up most of the bi-color pattern. Of course, not all tri-colors are marked alike, any more than all parti-colors or all bi-colors are marked alike. The same variations in color and pattern which occur in bi-color and parti-color dogs may be expected to occur in tri-colors.

The average black, tan, and white Cocker has an easily recognizable bi-color pattern with the two tan spots over the eyes and tan on the cheeks, inside the ears, and under the tail. The muzzle, legs and feet are usually well ticked with tan. The latest standard change in 1981 has been more specific about the markings.

Since tri-colors are basically bi-color dogs, they have the same ability as bi-color dogs to reproduce the bi-color pattern. Whether or not their offspring will have white spotting in addition to the bi-color pattern depends on whether the chosen mate has or carries the independent spotting factor as well as the bi-color pattern factors.

Remember, white spotting is recessive to bi-color. Tri-colors, therefore, represent a combination of two sets of independent genes, both of which are recessive in their manner of inheritance. When a

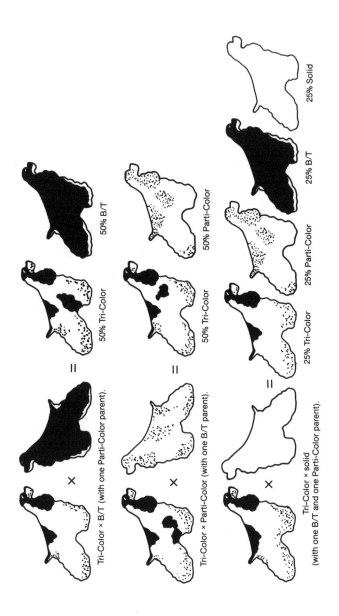

Figure 24. Tri-Colors

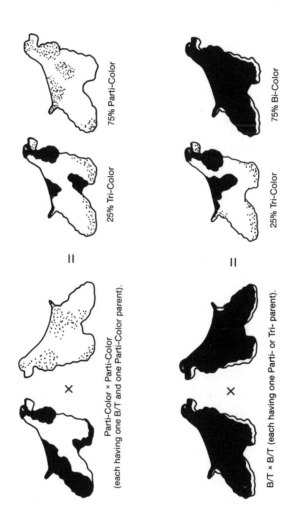

Figure 25. Tri-Colors, continued

recessive characteristic is visible in an individual, that individual is always homozygous (pure for that trait) and that individual can contribute only one kind of gene to its offspring. Therefore, it must breed true. Thus, when two tri's are bred together, they can be expected to produce only tri-color puppies. Whether the pups are black and tan and white, chocolate and tan and white, etc., depends entirely on what the parents are and what colors they carry recessively.

If tri-colors are desired, the bi-color pattern must be present in the pedigree and the white spotting factor as well. The only way to be certain that a particular animal has the ability to hand down to its offspring a particular recessive characteristic is by knowing that (1) the animal itself shows the characteristic; (2) the animal has one parent which shows the characteristic; or, (3) the animal has been test mated and has proven by its offspring that it has the ability to reproduce the characteristic.

The majority of breeders consider the combination of black (chocolate), tan, and white to be a bona fide tri-color. If the breeder wishes to produce this combination, he must make certain that the mating prospects have the black or chocolate pigment in their coat, for black and chocolate are dominant and must be shown by one parent before it can be expressed in the offspring. Any combination of colors known in Cockers may produce tri-colors provided both parents either show or carry the two patterns which are needed to produce the tri-color effect.

Figure 24 illustrates some of the many ways in which tri-colors can be produced, and gives expectancy percentages.

A word to the wise: By all means, use the black and tan and the chocolate and tan to produce your tri's. You may cross back and forth between the bi- and tri-colors at will. The bi-colors can help strengthen the pattern. Probably the most successful at this is the Trojan Kennels of Alice and Sheldon Kaplan of Texas.

Another method open to the breeder of tris would be to use buffs/reds which carry both the bi-color factor and the parti-color factor. There are many such dogs available. And while tri's coming from these dogs may be slower to appear, they can appear. By using this color combination the risk of too much black (chocolate) from breeding to the bi-colors will be reduced appreciably. For example, if a black and white (carrying the bi-color or tri factor) is bred to a buff/red (carrying the bi-color and parti factor), theoretically one out of eight puppies will be a tri-color. However, the other seven puppies will not be all mismarks and some of the parti-colors coming from such a breeding will possess the ability to produce tri-colors. Figure 25 illustrates the possible genetic combinations and results.

Mismarks

No discussion of color breeding would be complete without discussing the mismarked dog. All of us could empathize with the heartbreak of breeding a beautiful specimen and having it be disqualifiable because of improper markings. The standard is strict on this. It allows a small amount of white on the chest and throat without penalty but disqualifies a dog with white in any other area. Light-colored buffs where white hairs are seen from chest to chin intermingled with the buff are a problem. Their markings are *wrong*, and under the standard, they should be disqualified.

Just as it is possible to determine the relative amount of pigment formed by red or black parti-colors, it is also possible to compare the effects of these two coat colors in mismarked animals. Mismarking in Cockers occurs when white appears in certain areas which are usually well-defined and predictable. The feet, chest, and tail tip are the areas which usually show white. In addition, one frequently finds a white blaze or star on the forehead and a white muzzle in red animals.

Mismarked individuals may occur in the progeny of matings between two entirely solid colored dogs. In such cases they may, and usually do, represent modifications of the solid color type rather than true parti-color animals.

Mismarked Cockers can be produced in any of three ways (Figure 26):

1. They may be solid-color animals with a weakening of the ability to form or extend pigment over the whole body. This loss of the ability to form or extend pigment shows up by the formation of white (unpigmented) areas in those parts of the body which develop shortly before birth. This is why the feet, chest, muzzle, forehead, and tip of the tail are the areas affected. Animals which are mismarked for this reason usually, if not always, will pass on to their descendants the decreased pigment-forming ability which they themselves possess.

   In some cases, however, the decrease in power to form or extend pigment may produce so little white that ordinary examination fails to reveal it. The animal, therefore, appears to be solid-color and can be

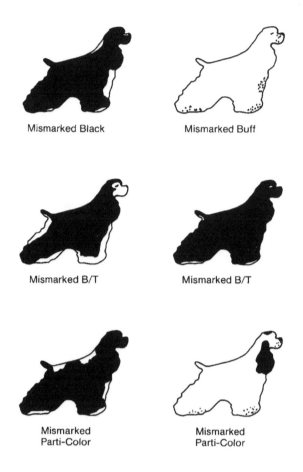

Mismarked Black

Mismarked Buff

Mismarked B/T

Mismarked B/T

Mismarked
Parti-Color

Mismarked
Parti-Color

Figure 26. Mismarkings in the three varieties

so classified. Thus, a few white hairs on the chest may be surrounded and covered by pigmented hairs and will not be visible by a surface examination. However, these animals are *genetically* mismarked and will transmit that characteristic to their offspring just as if they had more white.

2. A solid-color carrying a parti-color recessive may, or may not, be able to disguise the fact completely. If it can do so, it will appear just as a solid-color—as though it had no ability to produce parti-colors. Sometimes however, the parti-color pattern is not covered

completely. In these cases, white appears. Interestingly enough, it is again located in the "vulnerable" spots: the feet, chest, forehead, muzzle, or tail tip.

3. In some breeds, such as a Basenji or Boxer, a condition that would be considered a definite mismarking for a Cocker has become the common and established pattern for the breed. Such animals often "breed true" and give only offspring like themselves with few, if any, solid-color animals and few, if any, with large or irregular white areas. It may well be that some mismarked Cockers are of this type.

A breeder may wish to use a highly desirable mismarked specimen for breeding and that can be all right. However, the breeder *must* appreciate the consequences of such actions on future generations and proceed cautiously.

Cockers come in literally any color combination. A breeder may— if they wish—breed esoteric colors. Many people have tried. Sometimes these esoteric colors can be sold for a good price because they can be described as "rare." However, the trick is to breed good Cockers which conform to the current standard. "Rare" seldom means "correct."

CHAPTER 8

The Versatile Cocker
As a Show Dog

The show ring is where the Cocker has always excelled. The ringside crowds at all-breed shows are always larger when the Cockers are being shown. The breed with its variety mixture of colors and outgoing disposition has always been a crowd pleaser.

Developers of the breed wanted a small energetic dog who would be a willing worker with great stamina. He would need to have an outgoing disposition that could take anything thrown at him and still come back for more. The modern Cocker is all that and more.

The Cocker's head has always been his showpiece. Those large soulful eyes, the affectionate expression, and the long ears are the Cocker's trademark. So much so, that many a judge has gotten hung up on the head to the neglect of the rest of the dog. This type of judge is often called a "headhunter."

But there is far more to the Cocker than his beautiful head. He is a sporting dog par excellence. He still has the natural hunting instincts he was originally bred for. He is built to cover ground, to move up and through heavy cover and to flush, mark, and retrieve whatever game the hunter has chosen for sport. To accomplish these tasks the Cocker has to be built right. Previous chapters discussed the breed standard and how form should follow function. His function is to hunt upland birds and he has been designed to do that very well.

The Cocker competes in the Sporting Group at dog shows in America. In many other countries this group is called the Gun Dog Group. In still other countries he competes in a group exclusively for Spaniels. He is

91

placed in this competitive setting because he, like all others in this group, was bred for sport—to hunt/retrieve birds. Literally all members of this group have the same general demands made on their conformation.

If one were to take the Cocker standard—written to make a Cocker a good field dog—into the show ring, there is an excellent fit in what makes a Cocker a good hunter and what makes for a good show dog. The standard asks for the dog to be merry; that is, his tail should be going incessantly. That's easy for any Cocker. That outgoing disposition serves him in good stead. He wants to please at all times. The standard asks for a slightly sloping topline while moving. A Cocker built to go all day in the field comes with that built in. All in all, the standard describes a willing little worker who would just as soon work in the show ring as in the field or obedience ring—no phlegmatic dog he. The Cocker calls attention to himself by his willingness to show—to be *up*—to *ask* for the win. Properly trained, properly set down, a good Cocker is hard to beat.

The Cocker is one of the most versatile dogs of any breed. We have seen him in the obedience ring, we have seen him in the field, and of course around home as a loving family dog. Now let's look at him as one of the leaders in the show ring.

Even though Cocker registrations fell markedly during the 1950's and 60's, show entries indicated little decline. The earnest and sincere breeders hung in there while the fly-by-nights fled the breed. These dedicated breeders continued to breed top-flight show stock and the Cocker continued to get his due in the show ring.

The Cocker can be a true showman. With his coat of different hues and long ears sailing in the wind he is an impressive dog going around the ring. Cockers have been rewarded with some of the premier wins the dog show game has to give. While the Cocker is anxious to please and can become a fine showman, it does not happen without proper training and grooming and both take time and patience. Training your dog properly can make the difference between a winner and an also-ran. To insure you get words of wisdom about training I am going to quote one of the greatest handler/trainers of modern show dogs, Frank Sabella. Frank is now an AKC licensed judge. In his book (written with Shirlee Kalstone), *The Art of Handling Show Dogs*, published by B & E Publications, he covers all the bases in the early training of a show dog.

Introduction

Show training is so important that it becomes a part of the puppy's life. Training for the show ring should begin as soon as you purchase your puppy or from the time it is weaned, if you were its breeder. Especially with a baby puppy, your main objective is to begin establishing a pleasant, loving relationship which will become the basis of more formal training in the future.

Dogs are required to do two things in the conformation ring: to be set up or posed (and to hold that pose for an indefinite length of time during the judge's examination) and to gait (individually and in a group). While show training is not difficult, it does require time, patience, sensitivity and consistency on the part of the trainer.

Many people make the mistake of waiting for a puppy to grow up and then begin to train it. We don't mean to imply that some successful dogs did not start this way but, without a doubt, dogs that have the right kind of basic training as puppies are always the ones that stand in the ring with head and tail up, full of assurance. Just the repetition of correctly posing and leading the puppy will teach it to walk confidently on lead and to feel comfortable while being handled—and that's really what early training is for—to ensure that your puppy will grow into an adult that is confident and self assured in the show ring!

At what age should you begin training your puppy? Each dog is an individual and should be treated as such, so there are no "set" age limits as to when to begin basic or advanced show training. Generally, when you start basic training depends not only on your patience, sensitivity and consistency, but also on the puppy's capabilities and desire to accept being posed and lead trained.

Very young puppies are highly motivated by and responsive to their owners but, like babies, they have short concentration periods. Even though intelligence develops rapidly in a puppy, early training should always be started on a "fun" basis. Don't be in a hurry to start formal training too early; the first part of a puppy's life should be fun time and every dog should be allowed to enjoy its puppyhood.

Early Socialization Important

As the owner or breeder of a young puppy, you alone are responsible for its early socialization and training. Socialization can be described as the way in which a dog develops a relationship with its dam, littermates, other animals and man. Just as a youngster must receive a formal education and also learn to become a responsible member of society, so must you provide the best environment for your dog's potential to be brought out and developed completely. A young puppy is very impressionable and the socialization and training it receives at an early age sets the tone for its lifetime characteristics. If a puppy receives the proper socialization, is treated with sensitivity, patience and consistency, if it learns to be loved and respected, then it will always be happiest when pleasing you.

Earlier in this chapter, we mentioned that with a young puppy you want to begin basic training by establishing a happy and loving rapport between you and the dog. Pat and handle the puppy frequently, speaking reassuringly and using praise often. Let the puppy become accustomed to being petted and handled by strangers. A well-socialized puppy loves to make new friends and this kind of interaction between puppy and humans or other animals will be a prerequisite for the basic show training to follow. Hopefully, by the time the puppy is about 7 to 8 weeks old, it has learned a little about life. If it has been properly socialized, it is light-hearted and untroubled, because it has learned that it is loved and respected. Now it must be taught certain basics which lead eventually to more formal training for the show ring.

Here are some suggestions to consider before you begin basic training:

1. First training sessions should be given in familiar surroundings, preferably at home, and without noises or other distractions.

2. Make the first training periods short, not more than 10 minutes in length. As the sessions progress successfully, gradually lengthen each training period, but never more than 30 minutes in any single session.

3. If the puppy is restless or won't concentrate, postpone the lesson and try again the following day. Be sure, too, that you are not tired or impatient for the training sessions should always be relaxed and enjoyable for both of you.

4. Be consistent during the lessons. Use a firm tone of voice when giving commands. Some of the first words your puppy will learn in posing and lead training are "Come," "Stand," "Stay," and "No." Be sure you use the same word for the same command each time.

5. Remember that a young puppy is inexperienced, so be gentle and patient. Don't rush your puppy; give it time to understand what you expect and to learn how to respond.

6. Don't be too insistent at first. Puppies learn by repetition, correction and praise. Don't punish a puppy if it seems confused; instead, correct it until it does what you want, then offer plenty of praise. It is important that your puppy understand each training step thoroughly before going on to the next.

7. Always end each training session on a pleasant note and once again, give plenty of praise and perhaps reward the puppy with its favorite treat. A puppy can learn almost anything if given love and understanding.

Table Training

A grooming table should be one of your first investments, for it will be an indispensable help in establishing habit patterns. Most professional handlers, experienced exhibitors and breeders table train puppies at an early age because, aside from the convenience of having the animal at their working height, there is also an invaluable psychological advantage to table training (Figure 27). Even though the puppy is off the ground and experiencing a new situation, it is given confidence by the presence of its owner and submits to any handling or grooming, thereby establishing a rapport between the puppy and trainer.

It is easier to control a young puppy by teaching it to pose on a table...and recently, it is common to see judges using tables in the ring to examine other small breeds. On larger breeds, even though adult dogs are posed on the ground, early table training will be invaluable for teaching ground posing later on.

The majority of coated breeds require some type of regular grooming in addition to preparation at the show before going into the ring. Even smooth coated breeds need regular care. Early grooming training on the table will teach the dog to learn to relax. Later on, when the coat grows longer or the dog needs special attention, it will not object if it has to spend longer periods on the table and will rest and feel totally secure while being worked on. As a part of the training you should practice posing the dog at the end of each grooming session.

The table you select should be sturdy and covered with a non-slip rubber top. There are many different types of grooming tables: portable

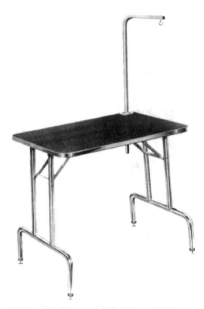

Figure 27. A grooming table is of indispensable help in training young puppies. The portable type illustrated here is covered with a non-slip surface and has an adjustable post and loop which can be removed when not in use. Portable tables are easy to fold up, making them convenient to transport to and from matches and shows.

(which fold up and are easy to carry along to matches and shows), adjustable (which move up or down) or a combination crate with grooming table top (these often have drawers between the crate and top to hold equipment). Some tables are equipped with a post and loop collar, which can be slipped around a dog's neck to hold the head up and keep it from moving or jumping off the table. If you do use a loop to give the puppy more confidence, never use one with any type of choking action. Never leave a young puppy alone with its head in a loop or standing by itself on a table unless you are sure it will stay.

Posing

You can start posing your puppy on a table as early as 6 weeks. In the beginning just stand the puppy on the table and get it used to being off the ground. Once this has been accomplished, then start positioning the legs in a show pose. Next, begin training it to be handled—feel its body, look at its teeth and let other people do the same. Experiencing all this at an early age will give the puppy confidence and make it used to being handled by strangers, which will be invaluable later on for the puppy's show career. If you persevere in the beginning you will discover that your puppy will never forget this basic training and later it will be much easier to work with.

When lifting the puppy for the first time, care should be taken not to frighten it. Don't come down too quickly on the puppy or attempt to lift it by grasping the back of the neck or picking it up by the front legs. Instead, kneel down to the puppy's level and let it come to you. Speak assuringly and pat the puppy if you can. Then using both hands to lift the puppy's front and rear, pick it up and place it on the table. Do be aware that a puppy might try to wiggle out of your arms so make sure you have a secure grip on the dog as you lift it and after you set it down on the table.

Be sure the table surface is not slippery and use the following method to pose the puppy:

Figure 28. Grasp the puppy with your left hand between the back legs and your right hand under the chest, at the same time giving the command 'stand' or 'stay'. When you pose the dog in the ring, in the majority of times this is the way it will be facing the judge. If the puppy fusses and does not want to stand, keep your hands in the same position and slightly lift the front feet off the table and put them down, then lift the rear legs off the table and put them down, doing both movements in a slight rocking motion. Repeat this several times to distract the puppy and get it to settle down.

Figure 28.

Figure 29. Move your right hand from under the chest and place it on the neck as shown, with the weight of the head resting on the top part of your hand. Don't grasp the neck too heavily; use a light touch, just enough so that you can control the puppy from moving to either side or out of your hand.

Figure 29.

Figure 30. Move your left hand from under the legs to support the tail and hold it in position as shown, so that the puppy learns to support its own weight on the table.

Figure 30.

Figure 31. Shows the puppy posed. These are the basic procedures for setting up the puppy. If you can accomplish all this in one session, excellent! Otherwise, work on the first position until the puppy assumes that pose without fussing, then go to the next position and so on. Each time the puppy assumes a correct pose, praise it lavishly. At all times when you are moving your hands to the various positions, be aware that the puppy might squirm and pull away, therefore you must be ready to recover it immediately by using the first position.

Figure 31.

Figure 32. To adjust the puppy's right front foot, control the dog by holding its head in your right hand. Release the hold on the tail with your left hand and allow it to grasp the right leg below the elbow and while pushing the puppy's head away from that foot, place the right leg down, then swing the puppy's head back into position to distribute its weight evenly again.

Figure 32.

Figure 33. To adjust his left front foot, with the puppy's head still in your right hand, reach over the dog with your left hand, grasp the left front leg at the same point you did on the right. Twist the puppy's head toward you (putting the weight on the right leg) and correctly position the left leg, then return the head to its normal position.

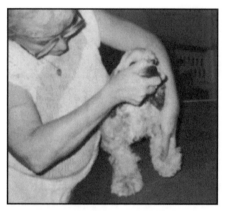

Figure 33.

Figure 34. If you have a dog with an excellent front, simply grasp the puppy under the neck, raise it off its front legs, then drop it back onto the table.

Figure 34.

Figure 35. To position each back leg, grasp the leg between the hock joint and foot and place it in the correct position. This procedure for positioning the back legs is used when you have the dog on lead or with your hand under the neck.

Figure 35.

Figure 36. The procedure for posing a puppy on a lead begins by following the same steps as shown in Figs. 32-35. Pick up the dog and place it on the table.

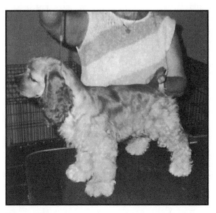

Figure 36.

Figure 37. Holding the lead in your right hand with the head in an upright position, move your left hand between the dog's back legs. If the dog moves its left or right front leg, position them as described before. Corrections to the rear are done the same as instructed in Fig. 35.

Figure 37.

Figure 38. Shows the dog posed in profile by lead and tail.

Figure 38.

Figure 39. If the puppy has a tendency to lean back when being posed, grasp the puppy under the throat with the right hand and place your left hand between the hind legs. Draw the puppy slowly backwards off the table, and then place it back on the table so that its weight is distributed evenly on all four legs.

Figure 39.

Figure 40. If a large puppy has a tendency to lean back when posed on the table, take hold of the tail and apply a pulling back pressure which will make the dog lean into its front. Later on, when the dog is posed on the ground, this method also may be used to correct leaning back.

Figure 40.

After your puppy learns how to stand properly, start posing it for longer periods of time. When the puppy can pose without fussing, the next step is to enlist the help of friends by having them go through the motions of lightly examining the dog—checking its bite and feeling the body—doing the things a judge will do in the ring. If you are training a male, in the ring the judge will check to see if both testicles are in place, so do remember to train your puppy to accept this procedure at an early age.

As the posing sessions progress, you can begin practicing the more subtle aspects of show posing, i.e., setting up the puppy in a variety of situations and on different ground surfaces, especially grass.

Author's Note: Special thanks to Wanda Towne of Townehouse Cockers for posing her puppies for these illustrations.

Lead Training

Of all the steps necessary to prepare a puppy for the show ring, probably lead training is the most important because there have been many potentially fine show dogs ruined by improper lead training. So many exhibitors wait until the last minute to lead break a dog then expect it all to happen in one try. Then they become impatient and treat the dog roughly and the puppy's reaction to all this is fear. Do remember that extreme patience is necessary because introduction to a collar and a lead can be a frightening experience for a young puppy.

Most canine behavior experts agree that at 6 weeks, a dog can have a small soft collar put around its neck. The younger the puppy becomes accustomed to wearing a collar around its neck, the easier it will be to lead train it later on. Begin by placing the collar around the puppy's neck for short periods of time and only while someone is in attendance. The first few times the puppy wears the collar, it may roll on the ground or try several other things to get the collar off, so never allow a baby puppy to be unsupervised. Make the first lesson short, not more than 5 to 10 minutes, then remove the collar, play with the puppy and praise it for being such a good dog.

After a period of about a week (or when the puppy is relaxed about wearing the collar) snap a lightweight lead onto the collar and let the puppy drag the lead freely about the floor. Allow the puppy to walk wherever it wants to go. If it starts to follow you, fine; but the first time the lead is attached, don't pick it up and jerk and pull the puppy in any way. After a few times of allowing the puppy to drag the lead around the floor, pick up the lead in your hand and let the puppy take you for a walk. Speak gently and walk wherever the puppy wants to go. Once again, don't pull or tug on the lead in an attempt to make the puppy follow you until it is completely accustomed to wearing the collar and lead.

When this has been accomplished, the next lesson is to try to walk the puppy on lead. The first time you try this, don't be surprised if your puppy pulls back or rolls over on the floor. Don't panic, just learn to be patient and speak gently. Put the snap adjustment under the puppy's neck at first so it won't be tempted to look over its shoulder or try to bite the lead. Squat down and call the puppy's name and the word "come" in your most inviting voice, to get the dog to move forward to you. If it balks or sits, try coaxing it to come forward for its favorite tidbit. You may have to give a slight forward pull to the lead to start the puppy toward you but remember, a slight pull does not mean a neckbreaking jolt for you can injure the neck and the puppy will associate the resulting pain with an unpleasant experience. If this is done several times without thinking, it can develop into a deep seated fear of the lead.

When the puppy comes to you, pat and praise it; then walk ahead with the lead in your hand and repeat this action to make the puppy move forward again. It should only take a short while until the puppy follows you. Eventually, the puppy will learn that if it obeys and follows you, there will be no pulling or jerking of the lead and that it will receive plenty of praise.

Once again, we caution that because a puppy's attention span is short, try to make each session brief, 10 minutes at most, then remove the lead, praise and play with the puppy. The main idea at this stage of training is to make the first lessons a "train and play" time that the puppy looks forward to and not something it dreads. After a few lessons, you'll find your puppy can be lead trained rather quickly and what is more important, that it enjoys the experience.

At this point, we want to offer some advice about early training. Always try to train the puppy to move on a loose lead to help develop its natural carriage. In the show ring you will be asked by many judges to move your dog on a loose lead and you will be prepared if you accustom your puppy to do it at an early age. When a puppy is taught to gait only on a tight lead, it gets used to leaning into the lead and without that pressure, feels completely lost. There is nothing harder to break than a dog that is used to leaning into the lead for support. Dogs that are trained on a tight lead also lose their natural head carriage and they often learn many other bad habits including sidewinding. In the ring, it is not uncommon to see exhibitors string up their dogs so tightly that the front feet hardly touch the ground. There is a trend to show certain breeds on a tight lead to make a more positive topline.

However, if a knowledgeable judge wants to discover whether the dog's topline is natural or man-made, he will ask that the dog be moved on a loose lead and, if that fault is present, it will be exposed.

While the puppy is being lead trained, don't train it to be hand posed at the same time. At first, these should be two separate procedures. Animals learn by repetition and, if each time you stop leading the dog and then get down and set it up, the dog will anticipate this action and will become discouraged from learning to stand naturally and pose itself without being set up by hand. So many exhibitors hand pose their puppies after each gaiting session and when this happens, a puppy soon gets the idea that every time it stops on lead, someone will bend down to hold its head and tail. In the ring, after you have individually gaited your dog, many judges will ask you to let the dog stand on its own. If your puppy hasn't learned to stand naturally at the end of its lead, it won't be able to do so in the ring.

As the gaiting sessions progress, teach the puppy to move on your left side (eventually the dog should learn to move on your right side as well as your left). Encourage the puppy to stand naturally at the end of the lead each time it stops. To help get the puppy to stand alert, try attracting its attention with a squeaky toy, a ball or by offering its favorite tidbit. Doing this will start to teach the puppy the fundamentals of baiting.

After a while you will be ready to begin more advanced training. Replace the training collar with a one-piece show lead or, on large breeds, switch from the training collar to a choke chain or a more substantial type of collar for better control. (As the dog grows older, remember that any collar or chain should be worn only during practice sessions and then removed to prevent the hair from wearing away around the neck.) Before starting advanced training, be sure that the lead is correctly positioned around the dog's neck. It should be high under the chin and behind the ears to keep the dog under control at all times. This position will also help to train the puppy to keep its head up because for the first few weeks, a puppy may need a gentle reminder under its chin to learn to keep its head up.

Next you should begin advanced training by teaching the dog to move down and back in a straight line. Once the dog does this well, then try moving it in a circle. As a prerequisite to executing the individual patterns, practice doing figure-eights because this will teach the dog how to turn smoothly. Then you can begin the other movement patterns that will be used in the show ring—the "L," the "T," and the "Triangle." Vary the movement patterns in each session and remember not to overtrain. Always end each session on a pleasant note and give the dog lots of praise.

As your puppy matures, it should learn to gait on grass, concrete floors and other surfaces including rubber mats (these are used at indoor shows). Once the lessons go well at home, take the puppy out and get it used to walking on a lead and being posed in new and different surroundings. Parking lots of supermarkets and department stores are excellent for this as there are usually lots of people and all kinds of distractions. For the first few outings, be patient and give the puppy plenty of time to adjust and respond to strange surroundings. Occasionally, because of a pup's insecurities, it may revert back to not being well trained for the first few outings.

The greatest pitfall for most young dogs seems to be going to indoor shows because the lighting is strange and the echoes inside a building can sometimes distract a young dog. The inside of a department store or shopping mall can help you to overcome this problem. Always try to anticipate experiences that might distract and frighten a puppy at a show and try to solve them while the puppy is young. If you live in a rural area and none of these suggestions apply to you, take the puppy to matches as often as you can for this is the best place to gain experience with the least amount of tension.

You must work with your dog to determine its best speed in gaiting. Each dog is an individual and looks best when moving at a certain speed and if you want to show your dog to its best advantage, you should determine that correct speed. Have a friend move your dog at varying speeds in front of a knowledgeable person to learn the right speed for your puppy. Then practice the movement patterns at that speed until the dog can do them smoothly. No dog can move at its best speed if the handler moves improperly, so you should take long strides when gaiting the dog. A common error of the novice is to move the dog too slowly. Short, stilted steps look clumsy and prevent the dog from moving smoothly. If you do not move fast enough yourself or with free and easy strides, you will prevent your dog from executing its most efficient movement. If you are showing a small breed take normal walking steps. For the medium or large breeds, move at a fast walk or run.

We should end the puppy lead training section with some advice about two common problems: sitting and sidling.

Sitting

When stopping, if you find that your puppy constantly sits, keep moving forward a few steps while attracting its attention at the same time with a piece of food or a toy, until the puppy understands that it must stand when it stops. If that does not work, bring the puppy forward a few steps, stop, then put your toe under its stomach to prevent it from sitting.

Another solution is to ask a friend to stand holding a long piece of rope or a show lead which encircles the dog's stomach. When you bring your puppy forward and it starts to sit, have your friend brace up its rear, but do not make this correction with a jerking motion. Breeds that sit when stopped are difficult to train to stand at the end of the leash with tail up (if that is desired in the breed). To remedy this, after you have trained the dog to stand when it has stopped, reach gently from a standing position and put up the tail, stroking underneath the tail until the puppy gets the idea of what you want it to do.

Sidewinding

A common characteristic during lead training is when a dog has a tendency to sidle. This can be caused by:

A. *The dog pulling away from you.*
   Solution: When the dog starts this habit on the lead or shows indications of doing so when moving individually, train the dog to move on your opposite side. In other words, if you are going away or coming back with the dog on your left side and it sidles, switch to going and coming with the dog on your right.

B. *A dog that has a tendency to look up at its handler while being gaited.*
   Solution: Never show a dog a toy or food while you are gaiting it as this can cause the dog to look up which may cause sidling. You can also try the alternate side method mentioned in (A) above.

C. *A dog is too short in back.*

Solution: If you move at a faster speed, it will go sideways to be able to move at a faster speed. The best way to deal with this problem is to get someone to move the dog at different speeds so you are able to decide at what speed the dog levels off. Another solution to sidling is to put two show leads on a dog and have one person walk on either side of the puppy so that the puppy walks straight in the center. If after a few tries you feel this method is working, the best way to keep the problem from recurring is by constantly alternating the sides each time you take the dog up and back. Gaiting next to a fence or a wall so that the dog can only move straight ahead is another solution to sidling.

Temperament

Temperament plays a major role in puppy training. While most dogs need consistent training to learn what is required of them in the show ring, some dogs are "naturals" at showing. They are outgoing and love being the center of attention and always seem to show themselves off to the best advantage. While these extroverted dogs are exceptions, they always train quickly and easily.

If you experience a temperament problem ("sound" shyness or hand shyness for instance), try to determine what is causing the problem and especially whether you might be the cause of it, as poor temperament can be the result of environment as well as from breeding. In the event you have purchased an older puppy that exhibits temperament problems, consider obedience training for that is a good way for an animal to learn regimentation and to get out among people. Obedience training has been used successfully on dogs that were kennel raised without adequate human socialization at the proper time.

Another part of training your puppy for the show ring has nothing to do with the ring itself, but a means of making going to the show a lot easier on you and the dog. This part of the training has to do with getting the puppy "crate trained." At an early age the puppy should be introduced to the crate that will be his home away from home. One of the best approaches is to put the crate down on the floor near where the puppy has his water bowl. Leave the door open. Put a favorite tidbit inside and let the puppy size it up. Most puppies will be somewhat leery of this new object. However, the puppy—by its very nature—is a curious animal and so will begin to approach it, at first giving it a wide berth. Now this process may take hours as the puppy, often unsure of what this thing is will leave the room for awhile before screwing up its courage and coming back. Gradually, it will approach closer and closer until finally it will be within inches of the crate. Typically, this is when the puppy stops short and reaches out its neck and head while keeping the body ready for flight if this "thing" should prove to be unfriendly. If nothing jumps out of the crate the puppy will feel safe to try to go further and eventually get the tidbit. However, staying inside, oh no, not me!

With this first success you know you have him hooked. Leave the crate down and pay no attention to it or the puppy. A couple of times during the day, place a tidbit in the crate. You will find it gone sometime later. After a few days of this game and you are sure the puppy (and not the cat!) is eating the tidbits, place a favorite toy in the crate. Let this game go on for a couple of days as well. Your next step is to gently pick up the puppy and place it in the crate with a tidbit inside and gently close the door. Be sure the puppy can see you as you go about your daily chores. He will most likely fuss about being confined. Talk to him, tell him what a great fellow he is and—if necessary—give him another tidbit. He should be confined for only about 10 minutes the first time. When you let him out, praise him lavishly for being a good dog. Over the next weeks you can extend the time slowly until the puppy comes to accept a few hours confinement as natural.

Once you have gotten to this point you can begin to let him sleep in the crate. Be sure you get up early enough so he will be let out of the crate before he soils himself. It's a good idea to put in some rough toweling or carpeting. Later on you might want to use a wire bottom or papering.

Next, you want to take him for a car/van ride to accustom him to motion. One of the trips to a shopping center referred to above would be ideal. Don't make his first voyage out into the world too long, however. Many puppies get car sick rather easily so keep the trip short and talk reassuringly to the puppy the whole time you are on the road. If people pull up along side of you at stop lights and see you talking to yourself, don't be worried, just put your hand up to your ear and they will think you have a car phone.

Grooming

Last, but not least in the preparation of a Cocker for the show ring, is proper trimming. In our family, my late wife Marjorie did the show trimming. I was shunted off to groom only the old dogs who would not be seen by the general public. This gives you an idea of my dog grooming skills. So, I turned to a real pro on Cocker grooming. Susan Kelley is a member of the Mission Valley Cocker Spaniel Club and the owner of the West Valley Grooming Salon in San Jose, California. Susan has groomed, shown and, of course, finished many of her own Cockers.

The most important thing to bear in mind when undertaking to trim a Cocker is time; be sure to have lots of it. Do not attempt to do your trimming at the last minute, or when you are tired or irritated. Patience is a prime factor. Be sure the dog is dry, thoroughly combed out, free of snarls, mats and body parasites before starting to trim.

The proper equipment will help to make the task easier. Most groomers use an Oster electric clipper with a #10 and #15 blade. Scissors are also quite important and a straight regular shears complemented by a thinning scissors. The kind with the blades on one side only, work the best. Be sure you keep your clippers oiled and the scissors sharp. A dryer with enough power to get through the profuse Cocker coat is also a necessity. Figure 41 shows a Cocker Spaniel before grooming.

Figure 41.

Use the clipper cautiously and only on head, ears, neck and shoulders; never on the body. Experience will teach you the proper method of operating the clipper. Use firm but not heavy strokes. Do not attempt to cover too large an area with any one stroke. Clipper burns most often result from working too rapidly thus pulling out hair, rather than allowing the clipper to cut it. A dull clipper will also cause burns. Keep your clipper in good working order; clean hair from the teeth after each trim job. Do the clipper work first and then bathe the dog and continue with the scissors.

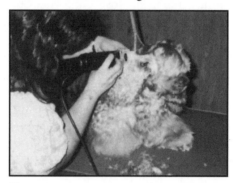

Figure 42.

It's a good idea to begin with the ears and clean out the underside and along the edges using a #10 blade, as shown in Figure 42. Experience will help you to select the appropriate time when to use the #15 and when the #10. For example, depending upon the way the hair grows and the thickness of the hair on the face, you may wish to interchange the blades to give the best effect. Use the #15 to clear out the stop coming down from the top.

Figure 43.

Once you have done the skull with clippers, as pictured in Figure 43, you should next work with thinning shears to "clean it up" and give a soft, rounded appearance. As shown in Figure 44, DO NOT get so close as to give the dog a scalped look. Be sure to leave enough hair on the sides of the muzzle to give whatever help the dog needs to give a square appearance. Figure 45 shows the desired appearance.

Figure 44.

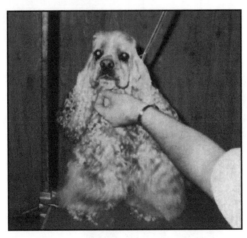

Figure 45.

The neck and shoulders are extremely important in a Cocker. After the rough work has been completed (as shown in Figure 46), you need to carefully look at how you will finish blending the neck into the shoulders. Lift and feather the hair along the juncture of the neck and shoulders as you cut it so it will lie flat and give a smooth look, as shown in Figure 47.

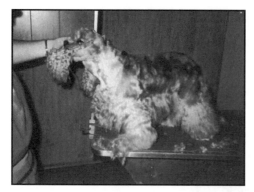

Figure 46.

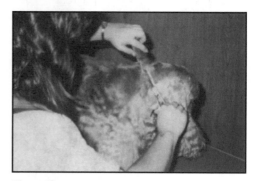

Figure 47.

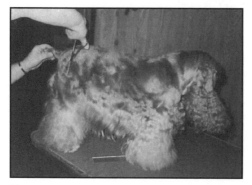

Figure 48.

The back should never be clippered. Flat-coated dogs present few problems—simply trim under the guard hairs so the coat lies flat and make sure it does not give the appearance of over-barbering. This is particularly true when you are attempting to thin out the hairs over the rump of a dog who is too high there, as is illustrated in Figure 48.

Dogs with the rougher or curlier coats present a different kind of a challenge. Try using the teeth side of your thinning shears to smooth out the coat. Be careful not to gouge—you are taking out all the guard hairs and poor workmanship will be quite apparent.

Think of yourself as a sculptor and try to imagine carving out the outline of the dog you want...it will go easier that way. Always remember that you want to take away excess hair and leave smooth lines. Get to know your dog so you can plan your work like an artist. There are certain areas that it's best to leave hair to cover up faults—i.e., a small dip just behind the shoulders. Other areas you may wish to take off as much hair as possible—i.e., the high-in-rump problem. In all cases, think in terms of balance. Don't trim to over-emphasize one area over the other. Remember, the dog "in proportion" is what the judge is looking for.

With that in mind, we move to the flanks. They should be well rounded and the hair should not fly in all directions when the dog is moving. This applies to the front legs and body coat just behind them. This calls for astute work with the thinning shears. Check your work as you go along. It's most helpful to have a mirror to check your progress. Don't try to thin it all at once. Take a little at a time and then check your work.

Thinning shears should also be used around the vent and down as low as the hocks. Watch that you do not cut in too deeply going down from the tail to the hocks. This can give the appearance of lacking muscle and depth in the dog's thighs.

Next, it's on to the feet. Clean out the hair between the pads (as shown in Figure 49) and cut the nails. Nails should never "clack" on the floor. It's a good idea to wrap a 3" X 5" card around the leg, securing it with a

Figure 49.

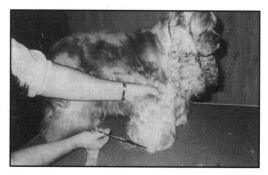

Figure 50.

rubber band just above the foot, so you can see the area you are working on. Trim the foot neatly (as shown in Figure 50), emphasizing a "cat's" paw look; round and firm. Once you have finished the four feet, take off the card and brush the hair down over the feet. Then, using the regular scissors, you should "neaten up" your work so the leg coat does not distract from the foot. Do not cut off the leg coat too far above the foot or the dog will look like he is wearing knickers.

It's a good idea to have someone gait the dog so you can tell if it will be necessary to stop or remove more hair to minimize his faults. For example, if a dog is out at the elbows, leaving a great deal of coat there will only emphasize the problem; if the dog has a tendency to being cow-hocked, leaving more feathering on the outside of the leg will accentuate this fault.

Our finished product is shown in Figures 51 and 52.

Beware of self-appointed experts; seek advice and constructive criticism from those with the knowledge and experience which qualifies them to help you. Do not subject your dog to the well-meaning, but often disfiguring, ministrations of another novice. The real professional who devotes his full time to the conditioning and showing of dogs is best qualified to render assistance in this respect. There are few handlers who will refuse to help the novice. Remember, however, that the handler has no way of knowing you seek advice and help, unless you ask him.

The photos on these pages are illustrative of the proper grooming techniques. For a more in-depth treatment of grooming read Mari Doty's "Trimming Guide." This can be obtained from the author at 202 So. Clovis Avenue, Fresno, California 93727.

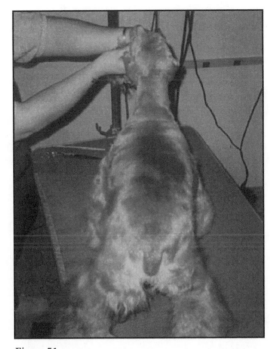

Figure 51.

Figure 52.

Ch. Caroling's Comet shown winning Best of Variety under breeder judge Marilyn Spacht. Handled by Gregg Anderson for breeder/owner Carolyn A. Calkins.

CHAPTER 9

The Versatile Cocker As An Obedience Dog

by Amy Weiss

Amy Weiss, pictured with Ch. Camelot's Confetti (Black and Tan), Ch. Camelot's Court Jester (Black), and two 7-week old puppies. Photo courtesy of Sacramento Bee.

It is with much enthusiasm that I urge you to enter the wonderful world of obedience with your Cocker Spaniel. Lucky you…you have perhaps one of the most responsive, intelligent and loyal breeds and, as you enter into a training program with him, you will make him a joy to own and a pleasure to live with.

Whether your aim is to pursue an active obedience show career, or simply to have a more controllable and livable companion, obedience training can, and should, be a most positive experience for both of you. In this chapter, I am going to discuss the formal part of obedience training, going for obedience show awards and training your dog to be the best type of companion.

The first step will be to locate the best training classes you can possibly find. While I don't usually recommend serious training for a puppy under six months of age, I've seen great results with younger puppies entered in a so called "kindergarten class." Here, the puppies are deliberately exposed to other puppies, sounds, smells, noises, etc., while learning gentle control from their owner. With the proper training methods and a good instructor, these early experiences can be invaluable. On the other end of the scale, it's just not true that "you can't teach an old dog new tricks." My Ch. Camelot's Cupcake, CD had a very successful obedience show career at 7 years of age!

Shop around for a good training class no matter what age your dog is. You might inquire of other breeders, contact the local kennel club or the local obedience club. Once you learn of a class, attend the first few times without your dog and observe the training methods used. A Cocker Spaniel is a sensitive, willing worker and you want your training done with kindness, love and respect. Most of all you want to use lots of praise. If you pursue a training program in this manner your dog will respond to you and be a happy, tail-wagging worker.

Many trainers have found that using food as a reward only for an exercise done perfectly can be a great training incentive. While this method may be somewhat controversial, I have found it to be of the greatest incentive in training my Cockers. Try to exercise thought and reasoning in your training. A Cocker thrives on gentleness and praise. Keep in mind what our standard preaches—"Above all he must be merry." Remember, his attitude toward this whole endeavor is learned only from you. A happy working, obedience-trained Cocker is a tribute to your training efforts and a wonderful advertisement for our breed. For those of you interested in showing your dog in obedience trials, the AKC Obedience Degrees are:

> CD — Companion Dog
> CDX — Companion Dog Excellent
> UD — Utility Dog
> TD — Tracking Dog
> UDT — Utility Dog Tracker
> UDTX — Utility Dog Tracker Excellent

To earn each of these degrees, your dog must score more than 50% of the available points in each exercise with a final score of 170 or more points (out of a possible 200) under three different judges, in at least three different shows. Obedience classes are divided into A and B classes. Let me break down the scoring for you.

The exercises and available points are as follows:

NOVICE (*To qualify for the CD Degree*):

Heel on Leash	40 points
Stand for Examination	30 points
Heel Free	40 points
Recall	30 points
Long Sit	30 points
Long Down	30 points

Novice A Class—The AKC Obedience Regulations state that the "A" Class shall be for dogs that have not won the title of CD and that a person who has previously handled or trained a dog that has won a CD may not be entered in this class. It's a true class for novices. No person may handle more than one dog in Novice A Class.

Novice B Class—This class is also for dogs that have not won their CD. However, dogs in this class may be handled by their owner or any other person. An exhibitor may handle more than one dog in this class. After you obtain your first CD on a dog, you must show all future entrants in this class. No dog may be entered in both Novice A and Novice B classes at any single trial.

Shirley Isola with Shirl's Donnie-Mite, CD. Shown winning First Place in Novice A at the Redwood Empire Kennel Club. "Donnie" scored 196 ½, earning his final "Leg" on his CD and defeating 26 dogs in the process.

OPEN *(To qualify for CDX Degree).* All exercises are done off the leash.

Heel Free	40 points
Drop on Recall	30 points
Retrieve on Flat	20 points
Retrieve over High Jump	30 points
Broad Jump	20 points
Long Sit *(handler out of sight)*	30 points
Long Down *(handler out of sight)*	30 points

Open A Class—This class is for dogs that have won the CD title but have not as yet won their CDX Degree. Each dog must be handled by its owner or by a member of the immediate family.

Open B Class—This class is for dogs that have won the title CD or CDX. A dog may continue to compete in this class even after it has won the UD title. Dogs in this class may be handled by the owner or any other person. No dog may be entered in both Open A and Open B classes at any one trial.

Ch. Charmary Consomme, CDX, TD and Ch. Dabar Agitator, UDT on the "Long Down." Owned trained and handled by Liz Doyle. Consomme was High Scoring Dog at the ASC Summer National in 1978.

Ch. Melodie Lane Mystique, UDT, Can. CD, TD shown retrieving over the high jump in the Open class. Owned, trained and handled by Billie Robbins.

Deidree Shannon Dodge, CDX, WD going over the broad jump in the Open class. Owned, trained and handled by Debbie Dodge.

Deidree Shannon Dodge, CDX, WD shown presenting the dumbbell to owner/trainer/handler Debbie Dodge.

Chidal's Something Special, CDX going over the broad jump. Owned, trained and handled by Joy Rosenbauer.

UTILITY *(To qualify for Utility Degree)*

Signal Exercise	40 points
Scent Discrimination (*Article 1*)	30 points
Scent Discrimination (*Article 2*)	30 points
Directed Retrieve	30 points
Directed Jumping	40 points
Group Examination	30 points

Ch. Dabar Agitator, UDT. Winner of the Dog World
Award in Novice and earned her TD at 1½ years of age.
"Aggie" has ten High Scoring Dog in Trails (eight at
Cocker Specialties and two at all-breed shows). Her chil-
dren are now being trained by their capable breeder/
owner/ handler, Liz Doyle.

Utility A and B Classes—A club may chose to divide the Utility class into "A" and "B" classes. When this is done the "A" class shall be for dogs which have won the title CDX and have not as yet won their UD title. The "B" class shall be for dogs that have won the title CDX and also UD (the latter may continue to compete in the Open B).

TRACKING (*To qualify for TD Degree*)

The purpose of the Tracking Test (as set forth in the *AKC Obedience Regulations Book*) is to demonstrate the dog's ability to recognize and follow human scent and to use this skill in the service of mankind. Tracking, by its nature, is a vigorous noncompetitive outdoor sport. Tracking Tests should demonstrate willingness and enjoyment by the dog in his work, and should always represent the best in sportsmanship

*Ch. Melodie Lane Mystique, UDT, Can. CD, TD shown
working the scent discrimination articles in the Utility class.
"Jennie" is owned, trained and handled by Billie Robbins.*

*Camelot's Second Hand Rose, Am. & Can. TD shown sur-
veying her tracking field. "Rosie" is owned by Lou and
Amy Weiss and was trained and handled by Billie Robbins.*

and camaraderie by the people involved. The regulations require that
each track be designed to test dog and handler with a variety of terrain
and scenting conditions. The dog is not asked to find the tracklayer, but he
must overcome a series of typical scenting problems and locate objects
dropped by the person whose track is being followed.

The Tracking Test must be performed with the dog wearing a harness
to which is attached a leash between 30 and 40 feet long. The length of
the track is to be not less than 440 yards nor more than 500 yards. The
scent to be not less than one-half hour nor more than two hours old and
that of a stranger who will leave an inconspicuous glove or wallet, dark in
color, at the end of the track where it must be found and picked up by the
dog. Tracking Tests require two judges for their conduct.

Ch. Melodie Lane Mystique, UDT, Can. CD, TD and
Seenar's Seraphin Sheaint, CDX, TDX, Can. TD. These
two black bitches are shown with their "tracking gloves"
and are owned, trained and handled by Billie Robbins.

With each entry form for a dog that has not passed an AKC Tracking Test, there must be filed an original written statement, dated within six months of the date of the Test, signed by an AKC-approved tracking judge certifying that the dog is considered by him or her to be ready for such a test.

TRACKING DOG EXCELLENT (*To qualify for the TDX Degree*)

The TDX Track shall not be less than 800 yards nor more than 1000 yards. The scent shall be not less than 3 hours nor more than 5 hours old and must be that of a stranger. Double cross tracks shall intersect the actual track at two widely separated points at right angles. The dog shall be challenged at several points on the track by changes in scent conditions. All types of terrain and cover, including gullies, woods and vegetation of any density may be used. Four personal articles shall be dropped on the track. Only the last article may be a glove or a wallet. The first article should be placed at the starting flag and be clearly visible to the handler. The 2nd, 3rd, and 4th articles should be dropped on the track at intervals and should not be visible to the handler from a distance of 20 feet.

The first Cocker Spaniel to earn a Tracking Dog Excellent Degree is Ch. Sandor's Coming Attraction, UDTX. She is a red/white Parti-Color who is owned, trained and handled by Judy Iby of Ohio.

It is said that "tracking is sport in the truest sense." The animal works for the sheer love of scenting. No dog can be forced to track. The tracking fraternity is known for its friendliness, its hospitality, and its encouragement to all participants. The thrill for the handler when the dog completes the test and locates the articles may be unsurpassed in any other AKC event.

It is possible for obedience dogs to attain championship status after they have achieved a Utility Degree. Obedience Trial Championship titles were approved by the AKC in 1977. Championship points will be recorded and any dog that has been awarded the title of Obedience Trial Champion may preface their name with O.T. Ch.

Requirements for the Obedience Trial Champion are as follows:
1. Must have won 100 points.
2. Must have a first place in Utility (at least 3 dogs competing).
3. Must have won a first place in Open B (at least 6 dogs).
4. Must have won a third first place under conditions 2 & 3 above.
5. Must have won these three first places under 3 different judges.

The points available are determined by the number of dogs competing both in Open B and Utility classes.

The first Cocker Spaniel to earn an Obedience Trial Championship was Ch. Mar Lee's Folly O'Blarney. He is also a red/white Parti-Color and was owned, trained and handled by Mary Whiting of Minnesota.

There are several non-regular classes offered for competition at some shows and trials. They include:

Graduate Novice	Versatility
Brace	Team
Veterans	

There are no degrees to be earned from competition in these classes. Scent Hurdle Demonstrations may be offered by any show-giving club, but they are not an AKC-recognized event. Obedience show classes are offered by dog training clubs, many all-breed clubs, and an increasing number of specialty breed clubs. It is interesting to note that many Cocker breeders compete successfully in both the breed and obedience rings. (Note that the previously cited O.T. Ch. Cockers were *both* conformation champions!) At the 1984 Mission Valley CSC Specialty there were 18 Cockers competing in obedience classes of which 11 were champions!

*Ch. Tabaka's T. Tissue Tucki, CDX and Ch. Tabaka's Tidbit
O'Wynden, CDX shown winning Best Obedience Brace in
Show at the American Spaniel Club National Specialty.
Owned, trained and handled by Ruth Tabaka.*

For more information, and in-depth explanations of each of the levels of obedience training and appropriate exercises, write to the American Kennel Club (51 Madison Avenue, New York, New York 10010) and ask for the *Obedience Regulations Book*. Single copies are free.

Now let's look at another reason for training your dog. There are many of you who won't want the formal competition of the obedience ring but want your dog to behave and be a good companion. For those of you who are interested in this aspect I would like to quote Curtis B. Hane writing in the March/April 1987 issue of the *Great Dane Reporter.*

Americans have always placed a high value on education. With students lining up for admission to colleges and graduate programs, schooling is again becoming big business. When it comes to their dogs, Americans are equally keen on education. Thus, the fields of obedience training, animal behavior modification, and counseling are also quickly becoming big business, offering countless services as complex as any university curriculum.

If you yourself are considering instruction for you and your dog, your choice must be an educated one. While some people harbor delusions of transforming the family pet into "Rex the Wonder Dog," your goals

Merlyn's Jasper of Camelot, CDX shown winning First Place for her first "leg" in Novice A at the Mission Valley Cocker Spaniel Club Specialty in 1983. Owned, trained and handled by Kim Steiner.

should be more realistic—teaching Spot not to pull your arms off when walked on a leash or competing in a local obedience trial. Perhaps you are part of a smaller number who have a serious problem—a dog that bites, barks incessantly, or has the family in such a state of upheaval that permanent separation from the dog looms as the only solution (witness the need for many dog rescue organizations).

Whatever the problem, you may consider seeking the help of professionals in solving it. With some basic knowledge and a bit of consumer investigation, most people can find a program that suits the needs of both dog and owner.

Most dog training methods can be roughly divided into two groups: (1) obedience drills and exercises; and (2) behavioral counseling and training (to correct such problem behaviors as chewing, biting, and jumping up). This is an informal categorization, however, as many programs do not fit neatly into either group, offering aspects of both types of training. Therefore, choosing the right training program for your dog must be done carefully. You'll want to consider your own goals and financial resources and your dog's needs if you want the best chance for effective humane training.

There are four methods of dog training most commonly considered by dog owners: (1) the do-it-yourself method using one or more training manuals; (2) kennels or schools that board dogs for a predetermined length of time for training by in-house handlers; (3) the private trainer or counselor who provides individualized instruction (often in the pet owner's home); and (4) group classes for both dog and owner. Each method has its benefits and drawbacks.

Dog Training Manuals

It is possible with the aid of books to train your dog yourself. While this method can prove effective and economical, it also requires a little more care both in planning and in execution.

First, carefully read, cover to cover, at least two books before you begin the actual training. Many books cover only basic obedience exercises. With a bit of bookstore or library searching, however, you should be able to find at least one book that deals directly with the problem behavior(s) you are experiencing with your dog.

Second, keep in mind that a group class outside the home method has the advantage of introducing your dog to strange sounds and odors and especially, other dogs. Should you decide to train your dog yourself, avoid practicing solely in the familiar and isolated backyard. Once you have your dog under control, it is usually best to move training sessions to a public park or an isolated corner of a parking lot. This is the environment the two of you will ultimately face, so accustom your dog to its surroundings early.

Two good training books are *Playtraining Your Dog* by Patricia Gail Burnham (New York: St. Martin's Press, 1980); *A Training Manual for Dog Owners* by the Monks of New Skete (Boston: Little, Brown and Company, 1978). These books deal with both obedience exercises and specific behavioral problems. A wonderful book on obedience is *Fido, Come!* by Liz Palika, published by Doral Publishing.

Kennels and Schools.

Dog boarding facilities that house your dog for a period of time and promise to return to you an "obedient" dog are often merely profiting from an owner's laziness or insecurity. The handlers may employ inhumane methods and return dogs to untrained owners who dishearteningly watch their animals quickly revert to their previous poor behavior within a matter of days.

While not a recommended method, if you do intend—for whatever reason—to leave your dog in any facility for training by a professional handler, be certain to investigate carefully. These operations make a great many promises. Don't be innocently drawn in by a free school bus service, recorded telephone tips, elaborate graduation ceremonies, and other costly frills.

First, visit several kennels and evaluate what you see, smell, and hear. Is there a noticeable odor? A well-run facility will be clean and neat. Do all fences and runs look and feel secure? Many dogs have escaped from poorly-designed runs. Listen for any sounds of shouting or confusion from the staff or tell tale signs of abuse or abusive equipment. Phyliss Wright, a former dog trainer, suggests a dog owner visit a facility at least twice before leaving a dog for training; three visits are not too many. Also, keep in mind that the "five-day quick train" method offered by many handlers is a myth. No reputable professional should offer or recommend such a program.

Second, it is essential that you insist upon follow-up sessions for you and your dog with the trainer. Any lessons the dog has learned will be wasted if the still uneducated owner returns to unsuccessful methods at home.

The Private Trainer

This method is perhaps the most effective means of correcting a dog's problem behavior. It is, for obvious reasons, also the most expensive, at $20 or more an hour. On the positive side, many private trainers are behaviorists who specialize in individualized programs emphasizing counseling for the owner and in-the-home instruction for dog and owner.

While most private trainers are reluctant to divulge their professional secrets, Mr. Bob Maida who operates a pet counseling and training facility in northern Virginia offers some tips he uses to stop destructive behavior:

1. Tie balloons on any area that your dog is chewing. When you see your dog near the area, walk over and casually pop the balloon.
2. Leave your radio on when you go out (no rock music—rock may make him aggressive) and turn on a light if it is or will be dark before you return.

3. When giving your dog verbal commands, change the inflection of your voice to a more powerful, no-nonsense tone.

Private instruction may be a worthwhile choice for all dogs but may be *essential* for some. Some dogs do not do well in a group setting, for example, aggressive dogs with meek owners. The disadvantage of a group setting, which often involves 15 or more dogs and owners is the amount of individual time that can be spent with each dog. Group classes sometimes cannot zero in on the person whose dog is having specific problems at home. By the very nature of such a class, instructors must come up with a universal method, a choreographed routine.

This individualized attention can be costly. Approximate prices can range anywhere from $50 for a two-hour session to over $350 for a complete program of behavioral counseling, in-the-home training, individualized lesson plans, and homework plans for the owner.

Two helpful books that explain dog counseling are *The Evans Guide for Counseling Dog Owners* by Job Michael Evans (New York: Howell Book House, Inc., 1985) and *Understanding Your Dog* by Dr. Michael W. Fox (New York: Coward, McCann & Geoghegan, 1972).

The Group Obedience Class

With the exception of books and manuals, the group class is certainly the most common method of dog training. However, when approached with the idea of training his dog in a group obedience class, the novice's first words may be: "But I want my Cocker Spaniel to stop jumping on visitors, not win a blue ribbon in a show!" True, most dog owners want to solve behavior problems and equally true, very few group instructors are behaviorists who have the time and expertise to address your specific needs. However, many dog trainers believe that obedience training in a group setting can both aid in the dog's socialization and establish a positive dog/owner relationship that carries over into behavior problem solving. When the dog misbehaves (for example, jumps up on a visitor) the dog can be told to "sit." If the classroom training has been successful, the dog will sit; thus the owner now has a means of communication through which he can make corrections.

"Whatever a dog learns in class should be transferable to the home. The goal is for the dog and family to live in harmony," says Phyliss Wright. She emphasizes the importance of dog and owner simply

A group of obedience-trained Cocker Spaniels in the Phoenix, Arizona area.

spending time together: "Obedience training gives the dog an interaction with you, and the more interaction you have the closer you become as companions. Training sessions should be quality time between you and your dog." By taking an active role in your dog's training, the bond between owner and pet is strengthened.

As mentioned earlier, when looking for an obedience class, be sure you observe at least one session before enrolling. An instructor who welcomes visitors is more likely to employ humane methods and enjoy working with both dogs and people. Carefully observe how the instructor handles dogs. Is a reward system used? Do not assume that all dog training instructors are, because of their daily involvement with animals, great lovers of dogs. As unfortunate as it may seem, some are in the business only for profit.

If you have decided to enroll yourself and your dog in an obedience class, seek the recommendations of any acquaintances who have attended classes previously. If you have difficulty obtaining first-hand information, don't head for the Yellow Pages yet! Check first with one or more of the following resources: (1) your humane society; (2) your veterinarian; (3) the Better Business Bureau; and (4) your local consumer protection agency.

Group classes designed specifically for beginners usually emphasize the rudimentary obedience skills: heel on the leash, down, down-stay, heel-sit, sit-stay, and come when called. The knowledgeable instructor, however, will attempt to deal, whenever possible, with specific behavior problems. Don't expect individual attention at every turn, but don't be afraid to ask questions and get involved. You will get out of the program only what you put into it.

The class will normally last from eight to ten weeks, one meeting per week. A knowledgeable instructor will stress at-home practice; set aside at least one-half hour (an hour if possible) for you and your dog to review the previous week's lesson. Also keep in mind that preliminary veterinary attention, particularly up-to-date vaccinations, is essential before exposing your dog to other animals.

Most good trainers endorse a training method with foundations in sound humane principles. They work to build a team…so the dog and owner have to work together, and they have to enjoy their work. Instruction should emphasize the practical benefits of training, always making a connection between class exercises and the home, yard and sidewalk. It's an excellent idea to explain to the class the purpose of the exercise.

As for the use of painful punishment devices, just about all the good teachers feel that anything that connects pain in the dog's mind with the owner should not be used. Positive reinforcement should be used. You don't punish your dog for getting on the sofa; you praise him for getting down. Praise and reprimand must be immediate: "Two seconds is too late. The dog will have forgotten already."

Let's look in on an advanced beginners program for adult dogs. This class is offered by a private training facility and held in the multipurpose room of a suburban YMCA.

Twenty dog/owner teams attend the Friday night class, the mid point in an eight-week series. Most arrive early to walk their dogs, to socialize, and to practice a few lessons before class. Terry, the instructor, stresses punctuality by closing the doors at the stroke of nine.

The class includes a wide variety of purebred and mixed-breed dogs and an equally diverse selection of owners, young and old, male and female. The owners attach training collars and long leads to their charges and take advantage of a short practice period, vying for space to put the finishing touches on that perfect heel. Terry, in a booming, no-nonsense voice, sets the class in motion, ordering the pairs to one side of the large and suddenly hushed room. Both dogs and owners are well trained in obeying verbal commands; the two-legged pupils obediently line up like happy recruits, their four-legged partners heeling at their sides.

The first lesson is "heel on a leash with turnaround," in which the dog must follow closely at its owners side while he walks several steps, quickly turns 180', and then continues for several more steps. Most of the teams perform this exercise with relative ease, with two exceptions. Terry helps one team by simply correcting the attachment of the leather lead and collar and encouraging those having difficulty to intensify practice sessions at home.

Terry then moves quickly to the next exercise: the dog must stand for examination while the owner stands three feet in front holding the leash. Next, as an added temptation, the leash is dropped. The dog must stand perfectly still; any foot movement is corrected immediately. When this exercise is completed, Terry gives the signal to praise, and an echoing chorus of "Goooooooood Dog!" fills the room.

As a final drill for the evening, the dogs practice their "sit-stay," their passive poses belying their eagerness to run to their masters for some well-earned praise.

As the class winds down, Terry explains the homework for the week. Teams are to practice the "go to place" lesson, which teaches the dog to go on command to a physically defined place, such as a rug or dog bed and lie down. After a few student questions, the class ends.

A final word…as was said in the beginning of this chapter, the dog is first and foremost a companion animal. As such, its training should make dog and owner better companions through close interaction. Achieving this simple goal need not be a painful or inhumane process. Finding the training program that meets your needs requires some legwork, knowledge, and a large dose of common sense. With the right program, dedicated effort, and respect for your animal companion, the rewards for both of you can be impressive. Your bonds of companionship, respect, and understanding will be strengthened, and most importantly, the home you share will be more comfortable for both of you.

The Southern California Dog Obedience Council holds a Top Dog Exhibition every year. The purpose of Top Dog is to provide an opportunity for the handlers and dogs who have earned the privilege to represent their clubs in competition for Top Dog honors. The success of this event relies on the integrity and good sportsmanship of the clubs, their members and the exhibitors. The winners of this competition go on to the California State Obedience Competition, and perhaps, eventually, to compete for the honor of the Top Dogs in the nation.

All member clubs of the Southern California Dog Obedience Council may enter a team in Top Dog. Most are all-breed obedience clubs with a few specialty clubs, including the West Coast Cocker Spaniel Club. A team is made up of two Novice, two Open and two Utility dogs. In addition, teams may also have three alternates, one for each class. The team is picked with the goal in mind of the consistently best working dogs, rather than the occasional high-scoring dog, as only the team score counts.

The 1984 West Coast Cocker Spaniel Club Top Dog Team. Pictured from left to right: Elaine Hansen and Ch. Kederdon's Derby, CDX; Todd Shuey and Sir Blake The Gentleman, CD; Roy Rosenbauer with Chidal's Licorice Kiss, CD and Chidal's Something Special, CDX, Marnie Wood and Ch. Glenmurray's Tally Ho, CDX; Lori J. R. Huff and Ch. Chidal's Licorice Prince, CDX; Col. William Mellen and Jet Jb's Jolly Rajah, CDX; Liz Doyle and Ch. Dabar Agitator, UD, TD.

The West Coast Cocker Spaniel Club has been proud to have had a team in this exhibition since the Sixties. The 1984 team proved to be the best placing team to date and the club members have the drive to continue to improve in years to come, as more Cocker exhibitors become involved in obedience.

Ch. Empire's Brooklyn Dodger

CHAPTER 10

The Versatile Cocker As A Hunting Dog

by Kenna Griffin
(formerly Chairperson, ASC Committee on Field Trials/Field Tests)

Cockers have been hunting dogs since the first hairy pads hit solid ground on the east coast. They hunted in England, and they were often among several breeds kept in American kennels for hunting.

With that kind of consistent use, it seems strange that the first attempt at instituting a field work committee within the American Spaniel Club would melt away from lack of interest, but it did just that. Frances Greer, writing in the ASC publication *A Century of Spaniels* reported that a committee chaired by A. Clinton Wilmerding was appointed in May of 1892 to study the sponsoring of field trials. No progress had been made by February 1906, and when Wilmerding resigned as committee chairman in 1911, the committee was dissolved. Yet he, and many other ASC founders, kept Cockers and other sporting spaniels and hunted them frequently.

The first field trial for Cockers and other flushing spaniels was finally held in 1924. Thus started a heyday for Cockers in the field, and it lasted until the next decade. Interest then waned, but picked up again in the 1950's, when most of the field-titled Cockers earned their field trial championships (FTChs).

An early promoter of Cocker field trials was Ella B. Moffit. In her 1941 edition of *The Cocker Spaniel, Companion, Shoot Dog and Show Dog*, she noted that "The first field trials for Spaniels were held on January third and fourth, 1899, sponsored by the Sporting Spaniel Club in

Charlie's Ebony Angel, UD holds one of her birds that earned her a WDX at the English Cocker Spaniel Fanciers of Dallas field test on May 12, 1984. She is owned by Heather Bartelme; Charles Palacheck was the judge.

England. It is noteworthy that both stakes were won by Stylish Pride, a 25 pound Cocker."

She dedicated her book, first written in 1935, to the memory of Rowcliffe War Dance, who contributed physical and hunting attributes to his offspring in the effort to re-establish Cockers as hunting dogs in the mid-1920's.

In her book, Moffit included in the chapter on "The Shooting Dog" some history of field trialing as well as training advice. She noted that it was 1903 before the first Cocker events were included in an English spaniel field trial. Two trials were held for Cockers in England in 1904; six in 1913; and eighteen in 1918. Two chief problems held back the sporting Cocker, she suggested: "First, the fancier's obsession for breeding for physical points without regard for brains, stamina and hunting instinct—the Cocker in short, had become an animal bred for exhibition purposes and a pet for the house. Second, the tremendous task of persuading the sportsmen of the desirability of the Spaniel in his pursuit of game."

Moffit included in the book a report of the first field trial for Cockers held, in 1924, in Verbank, New York. There were three stakes, with practically the same dogs in each. A. Clinton Wilmerding and William Hutchinson judged. Moffit's Rowcliffe Diana, acquired from Canada only two weeks before the trial, won the puppy stake.

"Only seven months old, she was so small that she provoked merriment from the gallery and I came in for my share of teasing," Moffit wrote. "Her only experience till she came to me was 'a few chases in the woods with her dam' in the words of her former owner. The masterful way in which she retrieved a full grown cock pheasant bigger than herself, turned the ridicule to respect and thus began a new era for the Cocker Spaniel in America."

Moffit admitted she was waging the war for field Cockers by herself. Others, she said, had wanted to change the breed's type which resulted in antagonizing many breeders. Her goal was to put the Cocker in the field as the breed existed, while trying to avoid dividing the breed into bench, field trial, and shooting factions, as the pointers had developed.

She described the hunting capabilities of a number of her dogs and others descended from them. She also noted, "The irony in the fact that, although we all admit that our ideal working dog should be a bit larger and a bit rangier than the typical show-type Cocker, we so often find the 'huntingest,' fastest and most intelligent to be on the small side. If someone has an explanation for that one, I would like to hear it."

Reports from ASC field committee chairmen reveal an overall view of Cocker Spaniel field trial history from the 1940's to the 1960's.

ASC Field Committee Chairman Ralph Craig, in the 1948 annual report, gives an indication of the trials and tribulations of establishing field activities for Cockers—something that never seems to change much.

The Field Trial Committee is happy to report that 1947 presented a more favorable picture of Cocker Spaniel field work and that continued improvement is expected in 1948.

Field trials were held in zones 1, 3, and 4. Zone 2 is the only zone where the interest has not yet developed to the point of actually

Ch. Carcyn's Chula Vista, WDX retrieving in water. This impressive dog is owned by Carlos and Cynthia Dominguez.

running at least sanctioned trials, where members can match their training skills in the competition of their dogs. However, in this zone several clubs have appointed field committees and it is hoped these committees will soon be able to start active work.

During the year the American Spaniel Club published an Elementary Spaniel Field Training booklet which was distributed to members, to secretaries of member clubs and to owners of registered Cocker Spaniels wishing to train them. Requests for this booklet have been received from every state in the Union and from England, China and Germany. Its effect in stimulating interest has already been noticed."

In the next two years progress continued, as is evident in this report in the 1950 Annual Report of 1949 activities, again by Ralph Craig.

Your field trial committee is happy to report the amount of progress which has been made in Cocker Spaniel field trials in zone 1 during the past year. Cocker entries have frequently exceeded Springer entries both in total entries and also in the important all-age stakes. In quality, there have been some outstanding performances and there are enough young dogs and puppies in training to ensure a steadily improving average quality for the future.

Two items in that report are especially interesting. 1) The comment about combined Cocker entries portends the Springer take-over in the field trial arena; and 2) a mention of the lack of interest in the midwest reveals no indication that it would become the most active area for Springer field trialing by the 1980's.

A 1952 report by field committee chairman Henry Berol made some interesting proposals:

> ...*a National Championship for Cockers;*
>
> ...*encouraging the idea of running a Field Dog Stake which we hope will lead to more interest in hunting Cockers in the field;*
>
> ...*and finally, but by no means least, I think the greatest accomplishment of this Field Trial Committee is the fact that the second oldest field trial club in the country, namely the Cocker Spaniel Field Trial Club of America, was taken over by a group of Cocker enthusiasts who, I am sure will do a real job for this club and keep its name before the public as one of the great field trial clubs of the country.*
>
> *1953 holds out great prospects for the Cocker Spaniel to become really famous in the field. It is the first time in history that there is a likelihood that a championship stake will be held this coming fall.*

This is the first mention, in an annual report, of a championship stake or trial. Berol proposed that holding such an official event, even though it might not be warranted considering the quality of the dogs' performances, would encourage more "cockerites" into participating in the field work. Over the years, this strategy has seemed to work but it has always been flawed because interest has never been sustained. Remember, the Cocker winning the National Championship earned the title of National Field Trial Champion as well as earning the FTCh.

The Field Trial or Field Dog stakes, by the way, must have been held by various clubs at their field trials and supported by the American Spaniel Club to encourage novices' interest in Cocker field work. The Field Dog Certificate probably was similar to today's Working Dog title. The year 1957 seemed to hint more strongly than usual of the lessening of interest. However much the ASC morally supported field activities, the limited number of participants had been the problem. It seemed no matter what incentives were offered, relatively few Cocker fanciers became involved in field work. For example, Berol in his 1957 report described ASC's next incentive plan:

The Field Dog Stake has rapidly disappeared, and I regret this extremely. Under the new ruling of the American Spaniel Club, a prize of $500 is being donated to the first dual champion, and a prize of $1,000 to the first triple champion. This should therefore interest a great number of newcomers to the field. I believe the ideal dogs trying for this dual or triple championship would come from the obedience class, rather than the bench class...They have a golden opportunity not only for enjoying their work with their dogs in the field, but also to obtain this large cash prize, which I am sure should tempt a great many people.

The $1,000 prize was never won. Probably it was dropped when the FTCh died. The $500 award was won by Ch. Minnopa's Mardi Gras UDT, a black and white dog owned and trained by Adelaide Arnisen of Jarretsville, Maryland. He finished his UD on August 20, 1961. His owner said she and his breeder, Ellen Waldner, took a cruise to Bermuda with the money. She didn't say whether Mardi Gras went, too.

"A nebulous dream until a few years ago, this first national event for Cockers, sponsored by the Spaniel Club, might be said to have been in the making since 1924," Berol wrote, and went on to describe that first trial much the same as did Moffit in her book.

Six years later when the first annual trial of the American Spaniel Club was held at Clinton, New Jersey, the ranks of Cocker enthusiasts had grown considerably. This trial included stakes for Cocker Spaniels, for English Springer Spaniels and a special class for any sporting spaniel in which there was one entry, in this case a Field Spaniel. The winner of the Cocker Open All Age was Howard Stout Neilson's F.T. Ch. Rowcliffe Gallant.

For the three years—1931, '32 and '33—annual trials sponsored by the Spaniel Club, were held on the Dix Hills estate at Huntington, Long Island. In the 1933 event, the Cocker All-Age winner was a bench show champion (later becoming a field champion as well), Herman E. Mellenthin's Ch. My Own High Time.

There was a long period when field trial interest in Cockers lagged, but it came back with a great rebound of enthusiasm during the middle 1940's and in recent years. It has risen so remarkably that it is not now uncommon to have 30 or 40 Cockers entered in a trial.

Dual Ch. My Own High Time.

In the national trial held December 6-7, 1954, the catalog carried this description, again probably written by Berol:

> *It is with considerable pride that we greet the Second National Field Trial Championship for Cocker Spaniels.*
>
> *The first National, also held at Herrin, Illinois in December of 1953, marked the first trial of national scope to be sponsored by the American Spaniel Club in its 73 year history. The running of that inaugural event, with 20 qualified starters, left no doubt that the Cocker had well earned the national fixture granted by the American Kennel Club. The stake was highlighted by keen and exciting competition through four land and two water series at the end of which the title was awarded to Camino's Cheetah, owned by H.C. McGrew of Fortuna, California, handled by J. Stanley Head. California also produced the runner-up in FTCh. Wildacre Harum Scarum, owner handled by Dr. J. Eugene Dodson of San Francisco.*
>
> *In 1953 at the English Springer Spaniel F.T. Association trial, the trophy for "Best Dog in the Meeting" went to a Cocker, FT Ch. Berol Lodge Glen Garry. This was the first time a Cocker had won the award in the 30-year history of the parent organization of the Springer Spaniel breed.*
>
> *During the nearly two decades when the Cocker was forgotten as a gun dog, through the magic of his personality he survived as America's No. 1 pet and companion dog. Today his qualities as a gun dog are becoming even more widely recognized. In the early hunting days in America, the flushing spaniel lost place to the wider-ranging dogs needed for the broad shooting grounds of the midwest and the south, and for market hunting. Now that America's hunting is confined more and more to restricted areas, the "comeback" of the flushing Cocker seems well assured.*

F.T. Ch. Camino's Red Rocket, winner of the Sixth National Cocker Championship Trial held at Lumberton, NJ, December 6-7, 1958. Owned by Clark Gable. Handler, Ivan Brower, who was also best amateur handler.

A third national trial was run in 1955 but this was hampered by severe winter conditions which cut down the number of spectators and the entry. The fourth trial was run in November of 1956 and W. Chalmers Burns, the ASC president, wrote at that time "The American Spaniel Club through its executive committee is fully cognizant of the incalculable value of the field trials and this national championship in establishing and maintaining the Cocker as a gun dog. To this end we have initiated and underwritten the financing of these national championships; we have a field trial specialist serving as our first vice-president; we have given every consideration and cooperation to the requests of the field trial committee; and we have given our name and prestige to these great National Championship Field Trials."

Even though the ASC lent their support, the years, from 1955 to 1962 saw a seesaw of interest. The field trials became a financial burden to the ASC and in 1962 they ceased to support the trials and they were abandoned. As has seemed to be the pattern throughout the history of Cocker field work, a small group of people were providing almost all the time, energy, money, dogs and entries it took to continue a field trial effort. In a 1983 analysis, Evelyn Monte Van Horn said, "It wasn't chance that brought the Cocker back to an eminent place in field trials. It was the result of diligent effort on the part of a few stalwarts who firmly believed that the Cocker's ability as a gun dog could and would survive."

"Today there are people who use Cockers as their favorite gun dog but whether there is enough interest to promote Cocker field trials, it is hard to say."

Cocker field trials "...faded for various reasons; among them, the limited number of breeders of field Cockers, lack of field Cockers to breed to, scarcity of interest," she noted.

On the positive side, when the ASC named Frank Wood of Norco, California, national field trial committee chairman in 1976, Cocker field activity increased. The Working Dog/Working Dog Excellent (WD/WDX) test was adopted and coordinated with similar tests given by English Cocker and English Springer Spaniel clubs. Though the requirements for passing a working test aren't as stringent as those for a trial, the dogs still must show ability and willingness to hunt.

Since the first working test was given by an ASC-approved club in October of 1977 in Connecticut, at least 36 WDX and 36 WD certificates—35 and 34 to Cockers, respectively—have been issued through 1984.

The Cocker Spaniel Club of Orange County, California held field training classes beginning in 1974, and has continued holding some classes and working tests since then. This club along with the Washington State Cocker Spaniel Club are among the very few clubs to actively participate and hold field events.

Many American Cockers have earned field titles participating in tests held by English Springer or English Cocker field tests. Other multibreed groups, such as the Maryland Sporting Dog Club, also hold spaniel field

Lady Rebecca D'La Swanson and Lady Melissa D'La Swanson pose with the trophies they earned at the American Spaniel Club Sanctioned B Field Trial, January 1984. They are owned and were handled by Pat Swanson of Tukwila, Washington.

tests in which American Cockers are welcomed. The Welsh Springer Spaniel Club of America has opened its sanctioned field trials to other spaniel breeds as well.

The ASC began holding working tests in conjunction with its national Cocker Spaniel specialties in 1978 in Huntington Beach, California, with the CSC of Orange County as the host club. Nine Cockers, four English Cockers and one Springer entered. Seven Cockers earned WDs and two earned WDXs.

In his ASC annual report that year, Field Trial Chairman Wood noted the number of certificates awarded and the 14 entries in the national attest to the fact that "our drop in the bucket of a few years ago has grown into a small puddle. Let's hope by 1979 we can grow into a pond...with another year or two under our belts, we could be ready to hold Cocker Spaniel Field Trials again. Wouldn't that be nice. After all, they WERE bred for the field."

He reported progress again in 1979. The second working test was held in July in Cincinnati, six dogs participated. One WDX and three WD's were awarded.

Wood related a typical experience of Cockers entering field tests for the first time, that of:

...Q-Bush Happy Leroy, CDX. This fine fellow, a mere 10 years young, astonished the gallery, not to mention his owner, Marjorie L. Quackenbush of South Weymouth, Massachusetts. You see, Leroy had never seen a bird up close before. He had never heard a gun shot, at least at close range, and I don't think he or his handler ever had so much fun together before.

Leroy charged out into the field on command and beautifully quartered on command. His CDX training really helped him here. When he found the bird he put it in the air like a veteran of many a hunt. The gunner downed the bird with one shot and Leroy didn't flinch but looked for another bird. Here came the advantage of his CDX training again. His handler stopped him with hand signals and sent him for his retrieve. He obeyed and went directly for the bird. But this time it was a downed bird. Leroy just wasn't sure.

Our judge, Mr. Dennis Blake of Orange, California, gave Leroy every opportunity to pick up the bird but Leroy wasn't sure he was supposed to, so he didn't qualify. After some exposure to downed birds, Leroy made one of the best water retrieves of the day.

The third national test was held, July 13, 1980, near Tampa, Florida. Charles Rowe of San Diego, California judged and awarded one WD and one WDX.

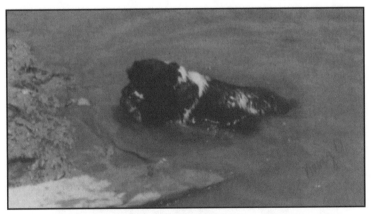

Diamond's Jacobus Jonker, CD makes his water retrieve to finish his WDX at the English Cocker Spaniel Fanciers of Dallas field test on May 12, 1984. He is owned by Sherry Creighton of Dallas. Charles Palachek was the judge.

In her report for 1983, ASC Field Committee Chairman Kenna Giffin announced the major accomplishment for the year:

"The most exciting news is that we've taken the first step toward reviving the field trial championship. The ASC is now approved to hold AKC sanction B field trials—the equivalent of B-OB matches. We had no trouble getting that approval."

Other achievements for 1983 included the first breed column featuring Cocker field activities to be in the *AKC Gazette*; allowing dogs earning field titles to receive ASC plaques and plates; and drastically increased communication with other Spaniel club field directors.

The next year's accomplishments included holding the first sanctioned match in January and the first trial in conjunction with a national specialty in July. Field dog and bitch classes were approved for the ASC Annual Flushing Spaniel Specialty. The ASC working dog program rules were clarified, and sections on philosophy and reporting procedures were added. Again, one of the *AKC Gazette* columns featured Cocker field news.

Late in 1984, the American Kennel Club Field Trial Department announced proposed rules for a master hunting spaniel title to be used after the dog's name on AKC pedigrees. Patterned after the master

The following photographs were taken at the January 1984 American Spaniel Club Sanctioned B Field Trial in Houston, Texas. They depict Pam Cullum Pena of Houston directing her sable and white dog, Lancer's Chardonnay, WDX in quartering and in following through with the retrieve.

Lance—making a retrieve.

Lance—fetching the bird.

Lance—returning to handler.

Lance—releasing the bird.

hunting retriever tests worked out the preceding two years, the tests focus on evaluating dogs as companion hunters rather than field trial perfectionists. They are similar to the working tests most sporting breed parent clubs have.

As the working test program grew so did the desire to return to some form of competition in field work. This was aided somewhat by the inclusion of special Cocker stakes at two English Springer Spaniel field trials in 1983 and 1984.

In 1983, the Washington State Cocker Spaniel Club's dedicated group of field fanciers, under the leadership of Ruth Tabaka, applied and received approval to hold a sanctioned field trial. The first one was in October of 1983, the second in April of 1984, and the third in September of 1984.

About the same time, it seemed only natural for the ASC to apply for sanctioned field trial status as well, considering the parent club's experience and resources. Again, AKC granted permission, and the first ASC sanctioned field trial in more than 20 years was held in January of 1984 in Houston, Texas.

The Washington State CSC opened two new chapters in ASC field history at two of their working tests by having the first Clumber Spaniel and American Water Spaniel earn their Working Dog titles.

In theory, it's possible for Cockers to earn a FTCh. Cocker stakes are allowed in conjunction with English Springer Spaniel field trials. However, only one open stake (for all dogs six months of age and older) is allowed at any trial, and it is doubtful a Springer club would give up its open stake to Cockers.

According to current AKC regulations, American and English Cockers are allowed to compete together to make up the six dogs needed for a Cocker stake. All pointers and retrievers, however, can run together in their respective trials. A number of spaniel field trial enthusiasts are working toward changing the rule to allow all spaniels except English Springers to compete in the same trials for FTCh wins.

Only the English Springers have licensed field trials now, and should other spaniels reach licensed trial status there is no desire to compete with the long-established English Springer trial system. Hence the move to establish an all-other-spaniel trial system.

English Cocker field fanciers are increasing in number and activity. The English Cocker Spaniel Club of America (ECSCA) working test rules differ somewhat from those of the ASC, as do those of the Welsh Springer Spaniel Club of America (WSSCA), and the English Springer Spaniel Field Trial Association (ESSFTA).

All spaniels usually are invited to participate in working tests and sanctioned trials sponsored by another breed's club. However, the working test score sheets must be sent to the secretary or field chairman of the appropriate breed club for a dog to receive a WD or WDX. English Cockers must be on the ECSCA score sheets and the ECSCA guidelines must be signed and returned. The other clubs accept each other's score sheets.

The first dog of any breed to win titles in three areas—about as close to a triple champion as it was possible to get at the time—was Dual Ch. Miller's Esquire CDX, a black and white American Cocker owned by Lauren Miller of Elgin, Illinois. He was whelped in 1938. He earned his field title in the spring of 1941, after having earned more field trial points than any other Cocker in 1940.

Another famous field Cocker was Dual Ch. My Own High Time, one of Herman Mellenthin's dogs. Mellenthin gave a memorial trophy in the dog's name for the annual Flushing Spaniel Specialty, with the stipulation that it go to the top Cocker being shown in the field and bench shows. Ted Young, Sr., renowned for his training, handling, and judging of field Cockers, retired the trophy at the 1955 show after winning three times, once with Ch. Tedwin's Lady Petite and twice with Ch. Tedwin Tommy Tucker.

Once again in 1986, due to lagging entries the Board of the ASC specified that the host club for the summer National Cocker Spaniel Specialty may choose, at its discretion, whether or not to hold a field event.

As frustrating as the attempts at keeping field work alive, it is worth the effort. The Cocker is a natural in the field and only needs an opportunity to prove himself.

Dual Ch. Miller's Esquire, CDX. Whelped 1/3/38 by Ch. My Own Peter The Great ex Ch. Miller's Peachie. Breeder/owner: Lauren T. Miller.

CHAPTER 11

Outstanding Breeders and Kennels

HERMAN MELLENTHIN—"My Own Kennels"

Many have called him "the father of the modern American Cocker." His forethought and planning produced Red Brucie, who marked the beginning of a new era in Cocker type and to whom the vast majority of today's outstanding dogs trace their ancestry.

It was no accident that produced Brucie, for Herman's experience in dogs dates back to his childhood. His program of breeding was started as early as 1912 when he maintained the Nihtnellem Kennels in Wisconsin. His kennel had begun to win with Cockers, but he also showed Collies and Airedales.

In 1915, he came east to live with Thomas McCarr and his wife, where he developed a love for trotting horses and began breaking and training them for Mr. McCarr.

He later went to Poughkeepsie where for four years he trained harness horses for Tommy Murphy, one of America's greatest trainers of the day. He often stated that it was his experience with horses that enabled him to be successful in dogs.

In 1926, he registered the kennel name "My Own" for his kennels at Poughkeepsie, New York and discontinued the prefix "Nihtnellem." As he was living in an increasingly crowded apartment, Mellenthin first came up with the idea of "farming out" dogs. It was that or have no room for living quarters for himself.

He set as his goal the breeding of a stud dog which would be the foundation of the modern Cocker. The Cocker Spaniel needed help badly when he began to seriously breed Cockers. He wanted to breed a merry, sporting type that was sturdy, yet small. He wanted spirit, cobbiness, ample bone, and substance. He envisioned a straight front, a dark eye. He wanted a bold dog, yet one readily amenable to discipline. He was very concerned that the Cocker Spaniels should be able to go in the field and do the work for which they were intended. He was one of the first to work toward establishing field trials for the breed, and he strove to produce specimens that could make their mark both in the field and on the bench.

In 1921, Mr. Mellenthin made a legendary trade whereby he secured Ree's Dolly, whom he bred to Robinhurst Foreglow, owned by judge Townsend Scudder. It was this mating that produced Red Brucie and from the first, Mellenthin recognized in him the type that was needed to produce the modern Cocker. A further description of Red Brucie is to be found in the chapter on "Dogs Who Influenced The Breed." This chapter also describes the "Big 4" litter out of Princess Marie which catapulted him to fame.

Herman Mellenthin's plan for a "new" Cocker had its roots in his long-range plans. As Ella Moffit said, "If it were luck, he would have a host of detractors; but even his greatest rivals in the sport of breeding of dogs admitted—even if grudgingly—that he was able to find combinations that were overlooked by others."

Ch. My Own Brucie

The next goal he set out for himself was to breed the "perfect" Cocker and he was certain he had achieved this in a black son of Brucie. He named this one "My Own Brucie." He had been holding this name in reserve until such a specimen came along. Ch. My Own Brucie, as we all know, is the *only* Cocker to have taken back to back Best in Show awards at Westminster. *(In point of fact, only one other Cocker, Ch. Carmor's Rise and Shine, has ever won Best in Show there.)*

Mellenthin always said that he got the greatest satisfaction in interesting others in the breed, in seeing them win, in helping them through pitfalls of breeding, more than in winning himself. He was satisfied in producing the good ones and letting others have the fun of carrying off the trophies.

Another of his major goals was to judge Best in Show at Westminster. He was able to realize that goal.

C.B. VAN METER—"Stockdale Kennels"

"Van" established the Stockdale kennels in California in 1927. However, he had a number of Cockers before moving to California from his home in Kansas City, Missouri. Prior to becoming interested in Cockers, Van bred Boston Terriers and a few other breeds. Both his schooling and breeding plans were interrupted by World War I but he resumed them both with a vengeance when he returned to Kansas City following the cessation of hostilities in Europe.

His first breeding specimen in Cockers was a red bitch but her career as a brood bitch was less than a rousing success. He had better luck with others.

Business brought him to the Central Valley of California where he first settled in Bakersfield. He played golf at that time at the Stockdale Country Club and it was an easy choice to make when naming his kennel. Van reportedly loved the layout and beauty of the club. It was in Bakersfield that he met Myrtle Smith who was to be his lifelong companion. She owned many of the great Stockdale dogs.

From Stockdale Dinah, one of Van's very nice original bitches, he obtained Ch. Bubble Up of Stockdale. She was sired by Ch. Sand Spring Follow Through. This breeding set him off on the path to becoming one of the top breeders of all time. Coincidentally, as was Herman Mellenthin, Van was also a lover of flowers. Orchids were his specialty.

Ch. Stockdale Town Talk

Stockdale's greatest success came in the Black variety. He spent many a long hour planning his breedings and laid out in detail the next two to three generations of his breeding program, He was a perfectionist when it came to the dogs. Capitalizing on some good western breeding, Van Meter concentrated on breeding beautiful heads and long sloping shoulders. He also wanted to breed that elusive "perfect" dog.

Van purchased Ch. Sand Spring Stormalong from the east coast and he became Stockdale's first true stud dog. He, in turn, produced Ch. Stockdale Startler who was famous for his bitch-producing ability. It was Startler's daughters that put Stockdale on the map. Fully 20% of Ch. Stockdale Town Talk's 81 champions were out of Startler daughters. Ch. Gaming Acres Maid of War, a Startler daughter, produced the first Cocker five-champion litter. A Startler daughter, Audacious Lady, was Town Talk's dam.

Names like Ch. Adams Black Perfection, Ch. Stockdale Red Rocket, Stockdale the Great and a host of others, came from the Town Talk and Startler crosses. Van believed that Startler had as much to do with Stockdale's success as did Town Talk.

Van was another who loved to help the novice. There is many a breeder in southern California who owes his or her success to the help of Van and Myrtle. His gentle guidance and encouragement make him and Stockdale a name to long be remembered.

BEA WEGUSEN— "Honey Creek Kennels"

The story of Ada, Michigan's Honey Creek Kennels, is the story of a very determined woman who set out to revolutionize the Parti-Color Cocker Spaniel. About the time Bea began her planning and showing, in the late forties and early fifties, Parti-Colors were the "step children of the breed." They had little coat, less substance and lacked the pretty features that first the Black and later the Buff color varieties enjoyed.

Honey Creek is the tale of the remaking of a variety. Before Bea was done, some 50 Honey Creek dogs had gained their championships. But, more than that, they won from coast to coast and in many other countries as well. Their producing ability is a matter of record, with literally all of today's Parti winners sharing a Honey Creek heritage.

Early on, Bea had purchased from her handler, Clint Callahan, Ch. Sogo Showoff, (then unshown) for the then princely sum of $1500. Eager to have offspring of her newly acquired prize, she bred him to Ch. Honey Creek Cricket (the dam of 10 champions). The breathlessly awaited litter

Am./Can./Cub./Mex. Ch. Honey Creek Vivacious,
Ch. Honey Creek Heirloom and Ch. Honey Creek Hero

Ch. Honey Creek Halo with Bea Wegusen

proved to be a shock as they were all undershot. Some months later Bea returned home from a dog show and her kennel man informed her that Showoff had climbed the fence and had bred Cricket again. In due time the litter arrived and this time all had perfect bites and one became the immortal Ch. Honey Creek Vivacious, the top winning bitch of her day. Not only did Vivacious win in the ring, she made her mark in the whelping box as well. With 14 confirmed champions she led the list of bitch producers for many years.

"Teddy," as she was called, made her debut as a puppy under judge Mrs. Shiras Blair to win the variety. She finished her championship under judge C.B. Van Meter. She made her debut as a special at the 1949 ASC show. Her record is history. She was shown by Ted Young Jr. at the start of his handling career, and was his first special.

Her first litter by Ch. Honey Creek Harmonizer consisted of six puppies...and six champions. Her second litter by her grandson Ch. Honey Creek Heir, also produced six champions. Her third litter by her son, Ch. Honey Creek Heirloom added two more champions to the list. A daughter, Honey Creek Halo, made her debut at the ASC in 1952 and won a five point major and went on to finish with all major wins.

At two weeks over one year of age, Halo became the first Honey Creek champion to go Best in Show at an all-breed event.

The foundation of Honey Creek was a birthday gift, Honey Creek Freckles, the product of a half-brother/sister mating. When bred to a son of Ch. Hadley's Trumpeter she produced nine males and two bitches. The two bitches were "Pennie" and "Flicka" and both produced champions for Honey Creek. Flicka became the matriarch of the kennel and every dog and bitch carrying the Honey Creek bloodlines descended from this grand red and white.

Close line breeding and inbreeding was practiced at Honey Creek with much success. judges raved over the quality and Bea's kennel prefix ruled the day. In 1950, Ch. Honey Creek Harmonizer became the top sire and Teddy's dam, Cricket, the top-producing bitch.

In 1952, Teddy returned to the ASC Specialty and again won the Parti-Color variety for the fourth time, a record unequaled. Of the 45 Partis entered, 30 were of Honey Creek stock. Of these 30, Teddy was either the dam or granddam of 21. The entire specials class was of Honey Creek breeding.

No mention of Honey Creek is complete without mentioning Norman Austin who campaigned many of the Honey Creek dogs to their championships and, in partnership with Bea, made Honey Creek a potent force in the Parti-Color variety for all time.

RUTH and ART BENHOFF—"Artru Kennels"

When asked to name the most successful kennel prefix in all varieties, the first name to pop up in the minds of most is "Artru." The Cockers of Ruth and Art Benhoff achieved unprecedented success in all three varieties with not only myriad champions but also with Best in Show winners in each variety. They established and perpetuated noted strains in both ASCOBs, and Parti-Colors and many winners throughout the country trace their lineage to Artru dogs. In Partis, "Available" and "Remarkable" are still prominent in pedigrees today and the Black and White Ch. Artru Ambassador went to Texas and created a very nice winning and siring record in that region.

It is from their efforts in ASCOBs, however, that the greatest achievements of all time for Buffs have been accomplished. Not only have their own breedings finished with such ease that it makes it look like child's

Ch. Artru Hot Rod and Ch. Artru Slick Chick

play to make up a champion, but the numbers of titled offspring sired by Artru dogs for others is overwhelming.

The ASCOB Buff strain began with Ch. Artru Crackerjack. He sired but one litter before his tragic and untimely death…a loss not only to the Benhoff's but most certainly to the breed. A grandson of Ch. Stobie's Service Charge and Ch. Gravel Hill Gold Opportunity, he managed—in this one litter—to leave behind a legend in the form of Ch. Artru Hot Rod. Twice a Best in Show winner at the ASC (1958-1959), Speedy also sired 25 champions including the influential Ch. Artru Johnny-Be-Good and his brother Ch. Jo-Be-Glen's Bronze Falcon. These two brothers provided a key for many of the winning Buffs of their time as the Johnny children, when crossed with Falcon daughters, produced champions for not only the Benhoffs but numerous others as well. With this combination, the Ted Klaiss' of Sagamore, produced winning bitches including the all-time top-winning Buff bitch, Ch. Sagamore Toccoa. Many other Cocker breeders benefitted from this combination as well.

Some years ago, Ch. Artru Sandpiper was the Cocker Spaniel sire of the year and he continued to produce phenomenally to earn his place in history. He currently stands #9 on the all-time list with 68 champion offspring. Ch. Artru Adventure, another Best in Show winner, sired over a dozen champions while Ch. Artru Red Baron, again a Johnny son, has continued to build on the Artru foundation and has added an imposing shrine of his own in the annals of breed history. He is currently #15 on the all-time list with 49 champion get. The leading producer for Artru is Ch.

Artru Skyjack with 87 champion get and the number is climbing. He rates at #8 on the all-time list.

Ch. LaMars London, also by Johnny, has himself made history of his own by consistently producing a distinctive kind of Buff that, in turn, seems to reproduce themselves with regularity. His descendants are noted for being well up on leg.

Ruth Benhoff felt that Baron was the most beautiful of the Artru dogs for his wonderful red coat and his very short back. But her favorite was Skyjack who carries three crosses to Johnny in three generations and six to Hot Rod. Incidentally, the Benhoffs had no bitches of their own to breed to Hot Rod and they had to start their own Buff line by taking puppies from his and other Artru studs to incorporate into the pedigree. The dominance of this kennel has always lain with the prepotency of the sires. However, let us not forget a little lady with the Artru prefix who is also listed among the breed's top producers: Artru Delightful II, the dam of 14 champions.

There is a further word on this success story. Actually four words: "hard work and sincerity." These are the keys with which they have opened the doors to their goals. From the planning of the matings, through the careful hand-raising of the puppies, the care and attention given them when not in the ring, the presentation of the dogs to the judges and spectators—and most of all—their willingness to help other breeders have earned them the respect of the dedicated dog fancy wherever the name "Artru" has appeared.

MARI DOTY—"Nor-Mar Kennels"

Mari and her husband, Norm, played a significant role in the evolution of the Cocker Spaniel. Their kennel, Nor-Mar, was well known throughout the land for its numerous champions. However, it is not the dogs alone that have made Mari famous. It was her role as Editor of the *American Cocker Review* that earned for her the niche in this particular hall of fame.

ACR was a voice to be reckoned with from the late 1950's until the early 1980's. On the pages of her magazine paraded the Cocker greats and novices alike. Her editorials and strong support of the research into cataracts in the breed was a major reason the work of Dr. Yakely, at Washington State University, was successful.

Ch. Nor-Mar's Nujac

ACR, due to Mari's artistic talents and her ability to write lucidly, set a longevity record that previous magazines like *The Cocker Spaniel Visitor*, *The Wagging Tail*, *Cockers Calling*, and *The Cocker Southern* could not emulate. Being an active breeder kept Mari highly involved in the day-to-day happenings of the breed. With strong support from her husband, Norm, the Nor-Mar prefix was a tough one to beat.

Mari's talent as an artist always appealed to me. She did a number of the sketches for my first Cocker book and has helped many an advertiser lay out their copy properly.

Though Nor-Mar is synonymous with Black and Tans and has gained recognition in Blacks, they have not done too shabbily in Parti-Colors, either—having bred 10 Parti champions. They have also exported dogs to England, Sweden, France, Portugal, Venezuela, Colombia, Mexico, and Canada.

EDNA ANSELMI—"Windy Hill Cockers"

I first met Edna in 1974, when I moved my consulting practice to New York City. Before leaving the west coast, I had asked Mari Doty about the people in the area where we had purchased a home, Westport, Connecticut. Mari told me to look up Edna and she would take me in tow. That she did. Edna and Ed Anselmi turned out to be two very warm and vibrant people who are very family oriented. Over the next few years we got to meet all the Anselmi children and to partake of Edna's bountiful hospitality. What a cook!

By the time we got to know Edna she was already a breeder of some repute. Ch. Windy Hill's 'Tis Demi's Demon was already well into establishing a name for himself and Windy Hill Cockers. I first met the next famous Windy Hill show dog and producer when this simply overwhelming Buff puppy came bounding into the room and took over. He was Windy Hill's Eagle Scout. Scout is now the sire of nearly 30 champions. I knew his sire, Ch. Bobwin's Boy Eagle quite well as I had judged him and given him Best of Breed on more than one occasion.

Even successful breeders have learned a lot from Edna about pairing up dogs to produce the best results. As Anita Roberts said "Edna has an 'eye' as to what looks just right. She follows a discriminate breeding program but has often said rather than to match the pedigree, she prefers to match dogs."

As is consistent with outstanding people in any endeavor, to be successful takes hard work. Edna began by working for a veterinarian to help pay for her hobby. She also learned to be an expert groomer. Many newcomers to the fancy have been the recipients of her knowledge and expertise.

Probably one of her great moments came—at the 1977 ASC Futurity —when a beautiful young Black and Tan, Windy Hill's Makes-Its-Point not only walked off with the Best in Futurity rosette but also scored for a

Ch. Windy Hill's Makes-Its-Point,
winner of 1977 ASC Futurity.

big five point major. Makes Its Point went on to become the sire of 20 champions before he died at a young age. He proved to be an especially valuable dog since he could produce tri colors. He has a number of champion tri-color grandchildren as well.

Today Edna is a well-known and popular judge. She has judged all over the United States and across Europe and Scandinavia. I have had the honor of being on judging panels with her and have also observed her from ringside. I am pleased to be able to include this astute women as one of the "famous people" who have made a significant contribution to the Cocker Spaniel Breed.

KAREN & VERNON MARQUEZ—"Marquis Kennels"

The Marquez's first litter was born in February of 1972. From that litter came their first champion. Ch. Tondee's Special Valentine. He was shown and finished by Dee Dee Wood. An auspicious beginning for a kennel which, as of date of publication, has produced 100 champions.

Ch. Marquis It's The One with handler, Ron Buxton

Vernon and Karen have specialized in black/white Parti-Colors although they bred a number of Blacks, including the 1987 BIS winner of the Annual Flushing Spaniel Specialty, Ch. Frandee's Forgery. The Marquez's give much credit to Dee Dee Wood and Bob Covey for being their early mentors in the dog game. They also feel that Annette Davies, Dottie McCoy, Norman Austin, Mari Doty and the late Bill Ernst were instrumental in their success.

Their greatest triumphs were Ch. Denzil's Super Daddy, who won the 1981 National Cocker Spaniel Specialty and the 1987 Best in Show win of Forgery at the Annual Flushing Spaniel Specialty. They are justifiably proud of Ch. Marquis It's The One, who with 3 Best in Shows, earned the #1 Cocker award—all systems—in 1985.

Vernon and Karen's Marquis Kennel also laid claim to an award that most breeders aspire to win just once—Top Breeder of the Year.

Marquis has won this coveted award in 1979, 1981, 1983, 1984 and 1985. That one is going to be hard to top. In the history of the breed only the Benhoff's Artru Kennel rivals that achievement.

LAURA and KAP HENSON—"Kaplar Kennels"

Kaplar got its serious start in California when they met Donna and Jim Pfrommer who had Ch. Essanar East Side. They bred their red Ch. Van-Dor Vermillion daughter to him. From that litter came two champions and their top-producing bitch, Sandrex Sangarita. Sangarita is the dam of the ASC Best in Show winner, Ch. Kaplar's Royal Kavalier.

While still in California, they bred Sangarita to Royal Lancer and that litter also produced some top ones, including Ch. Kaplar's Koka Kola.

My first introduction to the Kaplar "force" came when I judged a specialty in New Jersey. On that day, I put two puppies from the 6 to 9 Months Puppy Dog and Bitch classes to Reserve Winners in ASCOBs. They were Royal Kavalier and Kopi Kat. Both went on to great show careers.

A current special is Ch. Kaplar's Jiminey Kricket who is co-owned with Deryck and Christine Boutilier. Jiminey has done very well with his handler Greg Anderson. Jiminey is another Buff in a long line of Kaplar top winners.

The Kaplar Kennels are located in Frederick, Maryland—not too far from the Artru Kennels of the Benhoff's in Baltimore. There are many

Ch. Kaplar's Kelly Girl

similarities in the success stories of these two kennels. The Kaplar Kennel is located on seven acres, four of which are in pasture for their Appaloosa horses. There is also an 85 year-old barn on the grounds.

Their kennel set-up is small but workable with an intercom which pipes in music and keeps Laura in touch with the house. The runs are covered, and in the winter, heavy plastic runners are added for additional shelter.

The Kaplar name has been kept in the forefront not only by their great stud dogs but also by their great Black show girls. Kelly Girl and Kopi Kat are both Best of Breed winners and a host of others too numerous to mention have won top honors. To cap it off, Kaplar is well represented on the all-time top-producing bitches list with Ch. Kaplar's Kolleen, the dam of 18 champions (which places her #2 on the list) and Ch. Kaplar's Quicksilver with 10 champions (placing her #9 on the list).

BETTY DURLAND—"Dur-Bet Kennels"

Baldwinsville New York, a suburb of Syracuse is the setting of the famous Dur-Bet kennels. Betty, a graduate of Syracuse University with a degree in Zoology and a minor in Genetics, has put her knowledge to work to produce a line of dogs that is as well known in England and Australia as they are here in the United States.

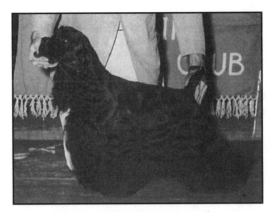

Ch. Dur-Bet's Knight To Remember

People are constantly amazed to discover that Dur-Bet is by no means a large operation. The emphasis has always been, first and foremost, to produce a quality dog of good temperament and health that can fill the role of an ideal family companion. The camaraderie that has been developed with pet owners serves a very useful purpose. "We get to see the development and eventual outcome of these dogs brought back for grooming and this is a very valuable experience in evaluating future litters."

A surprising fact, in a kennel known for its blacks and black and tans, is that the early Dur-Bet dogs were buff. A bitch, Tedwin's Tale had been purchased when the family lived in Albany. She was sired by Norbill's High and Mighty and was out of Little Buff Specially Me. In 1961, she was bred to Ch. Hollyrock Harvester. From this breeding came the top-producing bitch, Dur-Bet's Scandal Sheet. From her two litters by Ch. Jo-Be-Glen's Bronze Falcon, came Ch. Dur-Bet's Kristmas Knight, and in the second, Ch. Dur-Bet's Leading Lady. Leading Lady became the dam of nine Dur-Bet champions, including her first important black and tan bitch and another top producer, Ch. Dur-Bet's Tantalizer. This succession of top producers from Scandal Sheet to Leading Lady, to Tantalizer, and finally to Flirtation Walk was to prove to be one of the strongest bitch lines in modern history.

Kristmas Knight was Dur-Bet's first Best in Show dog but a liver ailment (that rendered him sterile) curtailed his possible long-term influence on the breed. As it was, in the four litters he was able to sire, he produced top quality. His most famous and influential offspring was Ch.

Dur-Bet's Nightie Night. Nightie deserves credit for transforming Dur-Bet from a buff kennel into one that excelled in blacks and black and tans. Nightie bred to Ch. Valli-Lo's Jupiter, produced three champions but her two breedings to another top winner and producer of the day, Ch. Hob-Nob-Hill's Tribute secured her permanent claim to fame. The first produced Ch. Dur-Bet's Knight To Remember, and the second, Am. & Can. Ch. Dur-Bet's Pick The Tiger, CD. These two boys and their closely-linebred girl friends account for almost 100% of the "look" of the Dur-Bet dogs of today.

Knight To Remember had a limited, but spectacular, specials career, winning the American Spaniel Club Show in 1969 and 1971. He became the sire of 33 champions including the well-known top producer, Ch. Shiloh Dell's Salute. He is also the sire of numerous English, Australian and Canadian champions.

Knight To Remember's kid brother, Pick The Tiger, became a top producer in his own right siring 27 champions including Ch. Windy Hill's 'Tis Demi's Demon, Am. & Eng. Ch. Windy Hill 'N Dur-Bet 'Tis Patti, one of the top winning American Cockers in English history, and Dur-Bet's own, Ch. Dur-Bet's Tantalizer, dam of eight champions. Tiger is also the sire of Am. & Can. Ch. Dur-Bet's Tiger Paws who has stamped his mark on present day Dur-Bet Cockers.

It is interesting to note that among the top producers in breed history are Demon, Salute, and Demon's son, Ch. Bobwin's Sir Ashley. Dur-Bet has, in many ways, moved alongside Artru, Stockdale and the other great kennels of the past in its influence on the breed.

BRIGITTE BERG—"Rendition Cockers"

Brigitte has had success with her Rendition line; most recently with Ch. Rendition Triple Play. His first big win was the ASC Futurity at 12 months of age. His litter sister Ch. Rendition Silk Stockings was BOS to Best Parti-color as well. Andrew's first All Breed Best in Show with Jane Forsyth came at 15 months. One month later he won BOB at the ASC Summer National under Carl Liepman.

Andrew is Brigitte's first homebred champion. He is producing consistently beautiful puppies that have been prominent in the last three ASC Nationals.

CHAPTER 12

Dogs Who Influenced the Breed

Every breed has had its famous sons and daughters. Some go streaking across the sky making sure that everyone knows about them only to disappear and not leave a trace of their moment in the sun. Others, perhaps not so famous, leave a lasting impression on the breed through their sons and daughters. These dogs stamp a breed with their greatness. They found a bloodline and thrust a kennel into the spotlight with their ability as a prepotent sire.

Siring ability can be passed down through generations. The most famous producing bloodlines in *any* breed is in the Cocker Spaniel. The lineage began with Ch. Hall-Way Hoot Mon, a black/white, the sire of 43 champions, to his red/white son, Ch. Scioto Bluff's Sinbad, the sire of 118 champions, and to his black/white son, Ch. Dreamridge Dominoe, the sire of 109 champions. There are already indications that Dominoe progeny will carry on this great producing strain.

There are many famous producers in our breed and it would be impossible to list them all here. Their producing records are to be found in the "Top Producing Dogs and Bitches" section of this book. This particular chapter will focus on key dogs whose influence made the breed what it is today.

Red Brucie

Mrs. Ella B. Moffit, in her 1935 book titled *The Cocker Spaniel*, wrote this about a pillar of the breed:

In 1921, Mr. H.E. Mellenthin rang me up on the telephone and asked if I would like to see a dog. I did not have to be bidden twice, knowing that this must be something very special. At first glance I was somewhat disappointed when he produced a three-month-old red puppy which he proceeded to set up on a projection alongside of his porch steps. To my dying day I will have a vivid mental picture of this "atom of Cockerdom." Not just a lovely puppy, as most of the best of them are at that age, but the impersonation of masculinity, Cocker Spaniel quality and substance from the tip of his nose to the end of his tail. Strong-headed, heavy-boned, short-backed, an exaggeration of every single thing that a Cocker should be. Perfectly delighted and thinking I had found what I needed to "found" the Rowcliffe Kennels, I asked him the price. "That is going to be the greatest stud dog the breed has ever known and he is not for sale," he answered me. And from this position, he could not be moved, hard as I tried. Little did we think, however, that those words would be so justified as they have been by the records. Sire of 38 champions, still a producer when 13 years old. Red Brucie will be in the pedigrees of the "right" American Cockers probably two or three times over and his influence is largely responsible for the "modern Cocker."

At maturity, he was not quite so impressive as a show dog, and for that reason did not make his championship. He was a little ahead of his time. He always was a strong headed dog (some might call it a

RED BRUCIE—"Brucie"
Whelped: June 8, 1921
Sire: Robinhurst Foreglow—Dam: Ree's Dolly
Breeder/Owner: Herman E. Mellenthin

little coarse) with enormous bone for his size and unprecedented short in back. His greatest gift to Cockers was long neck and lean, sloping shoulders with higher station and short backs. There is an amusing incident connected with his name. Mr. Mellenthin was still young in the breed and had not yet acquired a kennel prefix. He applied for the name of Red Bruce to the American Kennel Club, but failed to send a second or third choice. The name of Red Bruce being for some reason unavailable, the AKC exercised its privilege and changed the ending as it now stands. I remember the owner's disgust when the certificate arrived.

Probably Red Brucie's first outstanding accomplishment as a sire was the production of the "Big Four Litter." Ch. My Own Straight Sale, Ch. Rowcliffe Princess, Ch. My Own Peter Manning and Ch. My Own Desire whelped in 1922. The dam of these, Ch. Princess Marie, a very beautiful black bitch, of course merits a very large share of the credit for this wonderful black quartet. Straight Sale, acquired by the Windsweep Kennels, founded blacks for Miss Dodsworth. Princess, as the dam of Ringleader, founded solids in the Rowcliffe Kennels. Desire was a great force in the Sand Spring Kennels. Peter Manning remained with his breeder. To properly trace this degree of ability to produce, I think a study of Red Brucie's pedigree is important. Robinhurst Foreglow was a remarkable sire. Though naturally of the most importance in solid colors, he also had great influence in parti-colors, largely through his son Ch. Rowcliffe Red Man. All Spaniel fanciers should thoroughly appreciate the service that this great dog has done for the breed.

A favorite expression with some breeders trying to promote their own stud dog is that a certain dog is a "second Red Brucie." How stupid such a statement is. There will never be another Red Brucie, any more than there will be a second George Washington, or a second Abraham Lincoln. The times and conditions created circumstances which developed both of these great men as specifics. Likewise, the demand for a Cocker of a more sporting type gave Red Brucie his chance and he proved to be the specific for the need. People making such extravagant claims for their favorite only make themselves ridiculous by showing their ignorance. True, there will be other great stud dogs, but they can carry sufficient credit of their own if the facts make them so, without trying to borrow from the greatness of another—whose records stand where all who look and read may see.

Undoubtedly, to achieve greatness, a dog—like a person— must have the necessary opportunity. I am very sure that many potentially good producers, of either sex, have gone unproven to their graves. Such an opportunity unquestionably Red Brucie had. He first came prominently into public notice with the famous Princess Marie litter. He was just past a year old when this litter was whelped and, of course, it gave him a great send off. He was tremendously bred to. I do not believe that any dog was ever in such public demand as a stud. His popularity was enhanced, in 1927, by the birth of a litter out of Sweet Georgia Brown (breeder Thomas Carleton), which turned out five champions, a marvelous record for any bitch and showing the importance of giving the necessary credit to the dam as a producer. Thus out of 38 champions, nine came out of two litters!

Ch. Torohill Trader

Bain Cobb, of the famous Cobb brothers, reported in 1952 about his experiences with Ch. Torohill Trader.

It was back in 1933 when I drove over to the Torohill Kennels with Herman Mellenthin, with whom I was staying. Mellenthin had

CH. TOROHILL TRADER—"Trader"
Whelped: 1932
Sire: Torohill Trouper—Dam: Torohill Tidy
Breeder/Owner: Leonard Buck

purchased a young black dog for me to take back to the Blackstone Kennels of Leonard Buck (where I was to take over the management of the place).

As I recall, my first impression of the new young black dog, known to posterity as Torohill Trader, was of perfect balance; he was well upon-leg, and he had a head such as one dreams of. One of the first Cockers with large, very dark eyes, his expression was unusually soft and beautiful.

As he was immature and I felt he should be given a chance for body development, I waited a year before showing him and gave him plenty of road work with a German Shepherd Dog for a lead. What a thrill to see him move. Little did I know that this same movement was to leave an everlasting imprint on the breed. Even today the comment, "he moves like Trader" means that a dog has near perfect rhythm of movement combined with the old Trader gaiety and spirit.

Trader's first show was Morris & Essex where he defeated Ch. Windsweep Ladysman plus a huge class of current winners. This was the first of a series of wins which built for Trader a great career, more than a dozen Best in Shows, many, many Sporting Groups—and remember this—the groups at that time in the east were the strongest ever.

Trader lived with me all of his life and, as I enjoyed hunting and a good dog, it was only natural that Trader accompanied me on many a hunt. He was a natural retriever; his natural instincts for hunting were strong; he had a good nose. Fortunately he passed on those qualities and also became well known for his field get.

Until he died at the age of 14, he enjoyed life to the fullest extent. He enjoyed the show ring. Even his last appearance on exhibition at a Boston specialty when he was 11, he moved with such a proud and gay spirit that the ringside ovation was spontaneous with a tremendous admiration for the old fellow who could still give the young ones plenty of competition. Trader was a great producer and his many, many champions of truly outstanding quality built for him a monument. He will never be forgotten by Cocker breeders.

CH. TRY-COB'S CANDIDATE—"Candidate"
Whelped: 1940
Sire: Glidmere Buzz—Dam: Ch. Brightfield Delight
Breeder/Owner: Mr. and Mrs. R. Kenneth Cobb

Ch. Try-Cob's Candidate

Arthur Totton, a former president of the American Spaniel Club wrote in the September 1952 special edition of *Popular Dogs*, the following enlightening information about Try-Cob's Candidate and about the state of the breed in general:

> *In my opinion, the greatest progress was evidenced in the show ring and breeding of Cocker Spaniels just slightly more than a decade ago, and I am sure most of my readers will immediately think that I am referring to the popular reign of "My Own Brucie." I hate to disappoint and dislike to make comparisons, which are sometimes odious, but looking back to Brucie and what he did for the breed, I am forced to the conclusion that he was not the great dog we all thought him. In the days of his show ring triumphs he was outstanding, but sad to relate, it was not a very difficult task to be outstanding in a Cocker ring at that time.*
>
> *I don't think I take away from Brucie's glory by saying that he had a string of very easy triumphs. I don't get any kick out of pointing this out but I think it is necessary to prove that our progress as a breed actually began shortly after Brucie's heyday and that he had little or no part in it.*
>
> *Most of our progress I attribute to two dogs. Let me take you back to the American Cocker Spaniel show of 1941, which was held at the*

Roosevelt Hotel in New York City. I had a good seat, so I was present at the debut of "Try-Cob's Candidate." I am not going to say another word about conformation. I am simply going to say that we were electrified with the gaiety, the abandon of spirit; the gaiety fused with movement which seemed so absolutely effortless that it was like watching a perfectly trained athlete limbering up for some momentous event. I can remember so vividly, when Brucie and Candidate came into the ring for the judging—Brucie suffered so much by comparison when being gaited that I felt sorry for the old chap (mind you, up to this time, I had been a firm and staunch Brucie man). It was like seeing an old champ being knocked out by a cocky youngster. Very soon, sorrow gave way to elation in the realization that here was my fondest hope for the breed come true. After watching Cockers crawl around the ring on their stomachs, with their tails firmly clamped between their legs, shivering as if in the grip of some disease like palsy while being posed; let me tell you it was more than a breath of cool air on an arid desert. It was proof positive that we were afforded an opportunity of at last owning and exhibiting something in which we could have some modicum of pleasure.

I got a great kick out of the furor created at that time in the ranks and amongst the brass with regard to the merits or demerits of Candidate. I was a believer in what my eyes conveyed to my grey matter and was the first to bring a bitch over to the little house on Jericho Turnpike, but I was not the last; notwithstanding the calumny heaped upon the head of the dog and his owners by the experts. Bitches were shipped from all parts of the country and we were on the threshold of a new era. The Cocker began his triumphal march to the top spot in public favor. Exhibitors began to relax in the rings because they no longer had to be forever anxious about the gaiting or showing of their dogs. If they had Candidate breeding, they knew they had disposition aplenty and this does add to the pleasure of showing.

In my humble opinion, a dog to deserve acclaim must not only be a good animal himself, but he must be able to produce and so we have the evidence of Candidate's greatness written in the pedigrees of most, if not all, of the good ones today.

CH. NONQUITT NOLAS CANDIDATE
Whelped: 1941
Sire: Ch. Try-Cob's Candidate—Dam: Ch. Nonquitt Nola
Breeder: Mrs. Henry A. Ross
Owner: Ken Cobb and Florence Brister

Ch. Nonquitt Nola's Candidate

Quoting Arthur Totton again:

I would like to select one dog to which, I believe, I should pay particular tribute because of his influence on the breed and the joy he gave all of us during his show career. I first saw Nonquitt Nola's Candidate at a New Jersey specialty. He was in the puppy sweepstakes and, as far as I can remember, did not place in the money. Ken Cobb had the lead on a young dog belonging to Lawrason Riggs and as he was preparing him for the show ring he asked my opinion of his dog. I very truthfully answered; he was the best colt out of that stable that I had seen, but he left much to be desired when compared with the dog Tom Godfrey was showing. Very strangely, for a long time I thought I was the only man in the ranks who was in step, because I don't think the dog did any winning until the fall of that year. Thereby hangs a tale, which I cannot refrain from telling.

At that time, probably more than at any other in our day and age, there was a very strong little clique which exercised a considerable amount of influence in Cocker circles, and to say they resented the advent of this distortion or abortion (they called him much worse names than that) was putting it mildly. They persuaded Mrs. Ross of Nonquitt kennels that she really was doing a disservice to the breed by retaining in her kennels a dog which was so foreign in type and disposition. Mrs. Ross was influenced to the extent that she sold the dog to Ken Cobb without consulting Tom Godfrey. It does not require too vivid an imagination to picture the chagrin with which Tom received the news. As a matter of historical fact, he was trimming the dog in preparation for two New England shows when Ken arrived to take possession. Mrs. Ross was residing at her summer home but when telephoned, she confirmed the sale and Nonquitt Nola's Candidate was entered at both shows but under new ownership. He went Best in Show at one and won the Sporting Group at the other. Thus began a great show-winning career and another proof of his sire, Candidate's, greatness and influence on the breed.

Ch. Argyll's Archer

The story of Archer really begins with his mother, Sand Spring Smile Awhile.

Mrs. Constance W. Bayne bought Smile, bred and due to whelp in a week, from Mrs. L'Hommedieu. Smile whelped five lovely buff puppies. This was the start of Argyll Kennels.

When Mrs. Bayne looked for another stud for Smile, she came across a young black dog—Noble Sir, or Punch as he was called. Punch was the pride and joy of the George Kirtlands. He was a magnificently built dog and had all of the features that complimented her bitch. This breeding produced Ch. Argyll's Archer and Ch. Argyll's Enchantress.

Archer became the foundation of Stockdale Kennels and Enchantress became the foundation bitch for Nonquitt Kennels. Stockdale Kennels in California used Archer to sire Ch. Stockdale Town Talk. Not only a great show dog, Town Talk was for many, many years—until unseated by Sinbad—the top-producing Cocker of all time, with 81 champion offspring. The Nonquitt Kennels of upstate New York produced the great Cockers: Nowanda, Ch. Nonquitt Notable's Candidate, Ch. Nonquitt Notable plus a host of others. This breeding to Noble Sir started two of the most potent bloodlines in all of America.

From the time Archer was old enough to walk he was a perfect miniature of Noble Sir and hence acquired the name of Little Punch.

Archer's first show was the great Morris and Essex spectacular where he went first in a class of 15 puppies.

CH. ARGYLLS ARCHER—"Archer" or "Little Punch"
Whelped: 1936
Sire: Noble Sir—Dam: Sand Spring Smile Awhile
Breeder: Mrs. Robert W. Wall
Owner: Mrs. Constance W. Bayne
who sold to C. B. Van Meter

He was sold several times, first to Mr. Kirtland. He developed a chronic colitis and was very hard to keep in show condition. Mr. Kirtland sold him to Mrs. Suplee who sent him out on the show circuit. Because of his condition he did not win as much as he could have. He was a home dog and did not like the circuit.

The circuit ended up on the west coast, and there he came under the watchful eye of C.B. Van Meter. Van bought him from Mrs. Suplee. At that time he weighed only about 18 pounds, but with Van's expert care and devotion he very soon blossomed into a great show specimen. His show career with Van Meter was meteoric.

Van bred his Stockdale Startler bitches to him. This proved to be a perfect nick, his first champion being Town Talk; the rest of his career is a matter of record.

Ch. Stockdale Town Talk

Town Talk was the dog that put California in the forefront of the Cocker Spaniel breed. Until that time, all the action had been on the east coast. Town Talk was a showman and a producer. He was one of the first west coast dogs to journey east and take on the best. His Sporting Group

CH. STOCKDALE TOWN TALK—"Town Talk"
Whelped: 1939
Sire: Ch. Argyll's Archer—Dam: Audacious Lady
Breeder: Mr. and Mrs. S. T Adams
Owner: C. B. Van Meter

win at Westminster over the "best" the east had to offer was a turning point in western Cocker fortunes.

Town Talk was the creation of the clever mind of C.B. Van Meter.

Startler seldom sired an outstanding male but many good bitches. It was his daughters that gave Stockdale many of their top Cockers. A red Startler daughter, Audacious Lady, was Town Talk's dam. In fact approximately one-fifth of Town Talk's 81 champions were from Startler daughters. That's quite a nick.

Town Talk, like Red Brucie, changed the breed. The typical Cocker of the 40's and 50's was the so called "eastern" type. This dog was blocky in appearance with an average length of neck and a beautiful head. The shoulders were fairly laid-back. Many of these dogs matured young. On the other hand, Town Talk offspring were more up-on-leg and stream-lined looking. This was accomplished by having the shoulder rotated in a more upright position, thus giving a more sloping topline. His offspring also matured more slowly, being at their best at about 2 ½ years of age.

While Red Brucie was famous for his great litter of four champions, Town Talk sired an equally famous litter of five. Out of a Startler daughter, of course.

Ch. Maddie's Vagabond's Return

This remarkable dog came along in the 1950's to have a major impact on the inheritance of coat color in the breed. Until the 1940's, the breeders of buff and parti-color Cockers accepted the fact that they were breeding dogs that could not compete with the black Cocker Spaniel. All of the "good" traits such as flat bones, full coats, good rears, etc., seemed linked to the black color. In an effort to get these "good" features, the early breeders bred their stock to the blacks. They were able to get these features in their stock but unfortunately only in the black offspring. The buff and parti-color offspring still looked like the original stock. The advent of Maddie's Vagabond's Return heralded a new age in buff and parti-color breeding. Maddie came from a line where, a few generations earlier, a successful mutation had come about. According to Louis Schmidt, one of the best amateur geneticists of his day, a mutation which produced a dog which could sire like a black but in buff color had been produced. This dog bred true. Mr. Schmidt dubbed it a "dilute black." The dog they were referring to was buff in color but had black skin. He was black in type and in the ability to produce like a black. However, he could not extend his black skin pigment into his coat.

Maddie, as one of the top winning Cockers of his day, and with a fabulous coat, attracted the notice of many. With his ability to produce the

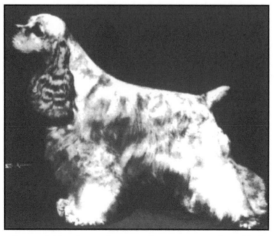

CH. MADDIE'S VAGABOND'S RETURN—"Maddie"
Whelped: October 1949
Sire: Poling's Royal Splendor—Dam: Lee-ebs Sweetie Pie
Breeder/Owner: Madeline E. Peuquet

light cream-colored buffs with coat and Black type, he was an instant hit as a sire. In his career he produced 60 champions. Perhaps his greatest contribution was to Parti-Colors. His Partis had dark blue spots all over their skin, which indicated they were dilute breeding and not straight Parti-Colors. The actual source of parti-colors in this line is not a Parti-Color dog back in the pedigree, nor a combination of Parti-Color dogs. In the dilution breeding, the color is so completely washed out that it is almost white. In the process, it is a normal and simple matter for the intense white color (recessive) to take over in spots, producing a parti-color with the colored area remaining a cream tan or light buff.

Ch. St. Andrea's Medicine Man

With the possible exception of my own Ch. Hi-Boots Such Brass, I think Medicine Man (Teddy) has to be my favorite dog. I first saw Teddy, in 1951, at a specialty show in Baton Rouge, Louisiana. He was handled by Ken Cobb and that day, under judge Bill Wunderlich, he went Best of Breed. He took the rosette in his mouth as he and his handler made an extra victory lap around the ring. I have never been so impressed with a young dog. We, at Hi-Boots, bred three champions from him and he is the grandsire of Ch. Hi-Boots Such Brass by one of Medicine Man's great daughters, Ch. DeKarlos Day Dreams.

Norman Austin, in the *American Cocker Review* in June of 1978, wrote the following about Medicine Man.

With the possible exception of Ch. Carmor's Rise and Shine, I do not believe there has been a Cocker Spaniel with which so many people have been emotionally involved as with Ch. St. Andrea's Medicine Man! His story and his influence have become legend. (Teddy died tragically at four years of age but sired 41 champions in his short lifespan.)

The first time I saw Medicine Man was as a puppy with his litter brother and sister, St. Andrea's Rain Maker and St. Andrea's Ragtime Gal. I was particularly interested in this litter because it was one of the first sired by Ch. Lancaster Landmark, a young black and tan dog I finished shortly after his sire, Ch. Lancaster Great Day. Great Day was a son of that incomparable black and tan bitch, Ch. Nonquitt Nowanda.

Nowanda came from an outstanding background and has become the matriarch of black and tan Cockers through linebreeding of her

CH. ST. ANDREA'S MEDICINE MAN—"Teddy"
Whelped: April 1950
Sire: Ch. Lancaster Landmark—Dam: Jubilo Madcap
Breeder: Ivan M. and Paula E. Wise
Owner: Major Ivan and Dr. Paula Wise

descendants, particularly in the Medicine Man family. Nowanda was an outstanding bitch and was the epitome of type. She carried a tremendous amount of body for her size but most importantly, she had style. These attributes she passed on to her children.

Medicine Man's story begins in Detroit, Michigan. Myrtle Haywood owned Jubilo Kennels and bred several colors, although dark red remained her favorite. When she decided to concentrate on reds only, she offered for sale the black and tan bitch named Jubilo Madcap. She was a Nowanda granddaughter and Dick Funk (Lancaster Kennels), who had always liked her, talked Myrtle into offering her for sale bred to Ch. Lancaster Landmark. Passage of time has proven this choice to have been very wise.

Madcap was sold to Major Ivan Wise and his wife Dr. Paula Wise in Vienna, Virginia. Dr. Wise, because of her European background, sentimentally chose the St. Andrea prefix for her puppies and did a beautiful job raising that litter. Soon they began to appear at puppy matches and in point shows, causing comment wherever they were shown.

It was not until I saw him with professional handler, Ken Cobb, at the New Orleans specialty show (Editors note: As I was also there that day I can attest to the fact that he went Best of Winners and narrowly lost to the great Ch. Benbow's Tanbark for the Variety) *that the full impact of Medicine Man hit me. When this marvelous dog walked into the ring, there was no doubt in my mind that here was true greatness with beauty, power and a driving movement beyond belief! Not until I saw the same qualities in Ch. Pinetop's Fancy Parade did I fully realize what a great asset and influence Medicine Man had been.*

A few telephone calls were made to people closely associated with Lancaster and bitches began to arrive for Medicine Man. William A. (Tubby) Laffoon, of Pinetop fame, was the first to have a litter by him because he had seen him prior to New Orleans and was quick to take advantage of what he saw!

The following year at the greatest of all eastern outdoor shows, the now extinct Morris and Essex Kennel Club event, the good fortune of those who bred to Medicine Man became apparent. In Cockers, judged by Mrs. Myrtle Twelvetrees, the Winners Dog, Reserve Winners Dog, Winners Bitch and Reserve Winners Bitch were all sired by Medicine Man.

Buff and Red breeders were almost thrown into a state of shock after the first winning by Medicine Man children. At that time the Varieties were separated, the Black and Tans were included in the ASCOB Variety, where they were most welcome as they helped to make points in a Variety dominated by Buffs. Occasionally, a young Black and Tan would come along with great promise but, for the most part, the Black and Tan's were plainer and lacking type compared with the Buffs. The Medicine Man children completely changed the Black and Tan image and Buff breeders scurried to reconnoiter. It was worth the effort as it pulled the ASCOB breeders together, resulting in a much better Cocker Spaniel.

The combination of Landmark and Madcap produced a composite of good traits. St. Andrea's Ragtime Gal was a good bitch and finished but the real quality was that belonging to the two brothers, Medicine Man and Rain Maker. The latter was a shade smaller than Medicine Man and perhaps a little more refined but he was a smoothly blended and beautifully balanced dog who did great winning on the west coast under the guidance of Roy Nelson. He left his imprint on the breed but with less impact than his brother.

Ch. St. Andrea's Medicine Man and Ch. St. Andrea's Rainmaker were the most influential litter brothers of the past two, nearly three decades (only Ch. Artru Johnny-Be-Good and Ch. Jo-Be-Glen's

Bronze Falcon rivaled them). They contributed to stabilizing consistency of type and balance throughout the country.

Ch. Elderwood Bangaway

Norman Austin, Bangaway's handler wrote this about him in the October 1956 issue of *Cockers Calling*:

> *Bangaway's children have established him not only as a great sire but a real contributor to our breed. Many a sire's champion children just fade away but Bang has been most fortunate in having his sons and daughters carry on with top wins across the country. It is almost unbelievable the number of Best in Show, Sporting Group and specialty show wins that his various sons have amassed. More important than the individual show wins, there lies the knowledge that his sons are carrying on his producing powers.* (Author's note: His son Ch. DeKarlos Dashaway sired the great winning and producing dog, Ch. Clarkdale Capital Stock, the sire of 76 champions.) *Shows today are represented by his winning children, grandchildren and even more recent, by his grandchildren who are the products of half-brother/sister matings. All of these, wherever they appear, bear a distinct resemblance to Bangaway—thus paying him the greatest tribute that I think can be paid to a stud dog.*
>
> *I know I am not alone in feeling great love and admiration for this wonderful dog. Retired at the height of his career, he went on to sire 45 champions. Those who renew acquaintances with him at Lazy Bend Kennels in Houston, Texas or are seeing him for the first time, all leave feeling it has been a great privilege to have shared a part, regardless of how small, in the life of this wonderful little dog that comes as close to fitting the standard of our Cocker, in my humble opinion, as any dog I have ever seen.*
>
> *Bang's admiration society started at a tender age, first by his breeders, Mary and Stewart Elder, later myself as his handler and a host of others as his career grew. Ranking foremost are his owners, Vivian and Bob Levy. Vivian who keeps him in such bloom that he could step into the show ring at a moment's notice. Those who know Bob Levy cannot help but admire him, not only as a fine man, but also respect his love and unique eye for animal flesh. It was Bob who found Bang and bought him the day he went reserve and not winners.*

CH. ELDERWOOD BANGAWAY—"Bang" or "Bangaway"
Whelped: June 1950
Sire: Ch. Myroy Night Rocket—Dam: Ch. Elder's So Lovely
Breeder: H. Stewart Elder
Owner: Vivian and Bob Levy

I shall never forget, that very same day, when he handed him to me with these words, "He is your's, treat him kindly." These simple words became the entree to one of the greatest experiences that will probably never be duplicated. Interesting too, it was more than a business arrangement…we became a family unit, united under the house of Bang.

Many people have asked me what made Bang stand out in particular. I admire his great heart, but I guess it was the overall balance and style that made him a champion among champions.

Many times I have suggested to those who have never seen him that they head down Texas way to see this remarkable dog. They would probably find Bob and Bang playing ball with a half-dozen of his champion children on the spacious lawns of Lazy Bend. He might even become to them, as he has to many, an inspiration or even a challenge to help perpetuate the shining name of Ch. Elderwood Bangaway.

Bang was a perfect example of the success of linebreeding. He was tripled up on Ch. Stockdale Town Talk through his great sons and grandsons, Ch. Stockdale Red Rocket, Ch. Myroy Masterpiece and Ch. Myroy Night Rocket.

Ch. Scioto Bluff's Sinbad

Sinbad, the dog that broke Town Talk's record by siring 118 champions, was descended, in part from the Honey Creek Kennels of Bea Wegusen and the famous cross (engineered by Jim and Beth Hall of Hall-Way Cockers) of Maddie's Vagabond's Return and Fraclin bloodlines. The Hall's Vagabond's Return breeding also produced Orient's It's A Pleasure, the sire of 104 champions.

Ch. Hall-Way Hoot Mon, the black/white sire of Sinbad, was a bit on the small side but was a born showman. Hoot Mon sired 43 champions, coming from a producing bitch line that was line bred to Ch. Maddie's Vagabond's Return, the sire of 60 champions.

Sinbad's dam, Ch. Scioto Bluff's Judy, was a great-great granddaughter of the fantastic producing and showing Ch. Honey Creek Vivacious. Vivacious, when bred to Ch. Honey Creek Harmonizer, produced a litter of six champions, one of which (Ch. Honey Creek Havana) was Sinbad's great grandmother. With this producing heritage it is easy to understand why Sinbad turned out so well,

I was fortunate enough to have seen Sinbad at the end of his show career. Ron Fabis brought him out to California where he went Best of Breed at the San Joaquin Valley Specialty, at that time the largest specialty show held in California.

CH. SCIOTO BLUFF'S SINBAD—"Sinbad"
Whelped: August 1959
Sire: Ch. Hall-Way Hoot Mon
Dam: Ch. Scioto Bluff's Judy
Breeder/Owner: Charles D. and Veda L. Winders

The Artru Dogs

I know this is an unusual designation, but the Artru Kennels of Ruth and Art Benhoff have produced so many sensational producing dogs that I am hard put to single out one that can be identified as "unique." I know Ruth prefers Ch. Artru Skyjack, now the sire of 87 champions, but when you have bred six of the top twenty producing dogs in breed history, how can you say one is best? Therefore I am exercising an author's prerogative in honoring all six of the dogs. They are:

Ch. Artru Skyjack	87 champions
Ch. Artru Sandpiper	68 champions
Ch. Artru Action	56 champions
Ch. Artru Johnny-Be-Good	52 champions
Ch. Artru Red Baron	49 champions
Ch. Jo-Be-Glen's Bronze Falcon	43 champions

When you add Ch. LaMar's London, a Johnny son with 54 champions to this list, you can see what an awe-inspiring producing power was concentrated in this kennel. No wonder Ruth was chosen Breeder of the Century by the ASC. There is more about the Benhoffs and their dogs in the sections of this book about famous people and top-producing dogs.

CH. ARTRU SKYJACK
Whelped: June 1971
Sire: Ch. Artru Red Baron—Dam: Ch, Artru Trinket
Breeder: Mrs. Arthur H. Benhoff

CH. ARTRU SANDPIPER
Whelped: July 1965
Sire: Ch. Artru Johnny-Be-Good
Dam: Ch. Bar-C-Kar's Peau Rouge
Breeder: Mrs. Corinne C. Karcher

CH. ARTRU ACTION
Whelped: August 1968
Sire: Ch. Artru Sandpiper
Dam: Van-Dor Fancy Triane
Breeder: Dorothy Vanderveer

CH. ARTRU JOHNNY-BE-GOOD
Whelped: January 1961
Sire: Ch. Artru Hot Rod
Dam: Jo-Be-Glen's Honeycomb
Breeder: E.B. and J. Muller

CH. ARTRU RED BARON
Whelped: June 1967
Sire: Ch. Artru Johnny-Be-Good
Dam: Artru Kathleen
Breeder: Mrs. Arthur H. Benhoff, Jr.

CH. JO-BE-GLEN'S BRONZE FALCON
Whelped: January 1961
Sire: Ch. Artru Hot Rod
Dam: Jo-Be-Glen's Honeycomb
Breeder: E.B. and J.F. Muller

Ch. Dreamridge Dominoe

Ch. Dreamridge Dominoe was whelped in March of 1968. He is the sire of 109 champions being surpassed as a producer only by his sire Ch. Scioto Bluff's Sinbad, Ch. Rinky Dink's Sir Lancelot, and Ch. Empire's Brooklyn Dodger.

As Ron Fabis wrote in the June 1977 edition of *The American Cocker Review*:

> *Dominoe has a "classic" pedigree. Sired by Sinbad, he is out of Ch. Dreamridge Dinner Date, a top winner and producer of nine champions out of nine pups raised.*
>
> *Dominoe finished his championship easily but was never specialed.*
>
> *A breeder once told us "Dominoe is like salt...most lines need a pinch of his blood for seasoning!"*
>
> *Actually, the Dominoe story begins with his sire, Ch. Scioto Bluff's Sinbad. Sinner was a cross between the old Honey Creek line through his granddam, Creekwood Miss Showoff (the dam of five champions), and the best of the Ch. Maddie's Vagabond's Return, and Merlady lines. Honey Creek was famous for beautiful plush red and whites with large, expressive eyes and abundant coats. His sire, Ch. Hall-Way Hoot Mon, was a very stable, showy black and white—small, sound and typey. Moving back a few years, Ch.*

CH. DREAMRIDGE DOMINOE—"Dominoe"
Whelped: March 1968
Sire: Ch. Scioto Bluffs Sinbad
Dam: Ch. Dreamridge Dinner Date
Breeder/Owner: Thomas F. O'Neal

Dau-Han Dan Morgan (the sire of 29 champions) was noted for producing proper expressions, skulls and beautiful muzzles. His daughter, Ch. Pounette Fancy Dancer was one of the most beautiful bitches of her day. Bred to Sinbad, she produced Pounette Perrette (the dam of 10 champions), the foundation bitch of Dreamridge. When bred to Ch. Clarkdale Calcutta, the sire of 33 champions and a strong stallion-type of a male, she produced Dinner Date. Dinner Date still personifies the standard for Tom O'Neal and Ron Fabis, the one-two punch of Dreamridge. Dinner Date was a great bitch with proper muzzle, dome and eyes. She had long, well laid-back shoulders, was short coupled with a strong rear and showmanship to burn. I saw her years ago when Ron brought her out to the San Joaquin Valley CSC, and was much impressed.

She was bred back to Sinbad, her grandsire, to intensify the bloodlines, This mating produced Dominoe, the rest is history.

Ch. Windy Hill's 'Tis Demi's Demon

I asked Anita Roberts of Memoirs' fame, a close friend of Edna Anselmi, the mistress of Windy Hill, to give me her recollections of Demon. Windy Hill is a name that has become synonymous with quality Cockers in black and tan, black and buff.

The foundation for the Windy Hill line was laid when Edna purchased a red bitch named Tracey from Liz Gorr of Stonehedge Kennels.

Tracey was a beautifully headed and sound bodied bitch who helped to found the Windy Hill line. Quoting from Marcus Aurelius, "That which comes after, ever conforms to that which has gone before," was a perfect expression for Tracey who lived a long and healthy life.

Of the many fine dogs who have sported the Windy Hill prefix, Ch. Windy Hill's 'Tis Demi's Demon (or "Demon" as he was known to all), has exerted the most influence. He is known for his multiple-champion litters and, to date, his record stands at 83 champions—placing him sixth on the all-time producing list. Amazingly enough, his black son, Ch. Bobwin's Sir Ashley is the sire of 65 champions. Ashley is one of the six champions of Ashley's Cherry Jubilee.

Demon was sired by Ch. Dur-Bets Pick the Tiger, CD—the sire of 26 champions himself. In turn, Pick the Tiger's sire is Ch. Hob-Nob Hill's Tribute, the sire of 54 champions, Tribute's grandsire, Ch. Merryhaven Strutaway, produced 28 champion offspring.

CH. WINDY HILL'S 'TIS DEMI'S DEMON—"Demon"
Whelped: May 1972
Sire: Ch. Dur-Bet's Pick The Tiger, CD
Dam: Ch. Windy Hill's 'Tis Demi-Tasse
Breeder: Edna T. Anselmi

Demon's dam, Ch. Windy Hill's 'Tis Demi Tasse was also the dam of the famous Ch. Windy Hill Makes-Its-Point, the winner of the 1977 ASC Futurity. Makes-Its-Point was the sire of 20 champions when he met an early and untimely death.

Carol Hilder of Carlens Cockers fell in love with Demon as a youngster and took him home for a few months. While in her charge, he was brought to California to try his luck at the famous San Joaquin Valley CSC Specialty. It was there he earned his first blue ribbon. After returning east, he won the Sweepstakes at the Maryland Specialty. He then returned home to Windy Hill and quickly finished his championship.

The first litters sired by Demon demonstrated his dominance in passing on substance, conformation, and lovely heads to his offspring when bred to almost any bloodline. But most of all, Demon was a gentleman with an unsurpassed disposition. When standing at stud at Memoirs, he jumped from a grooming table and suffered a nasty break in his leg and shoulder. Only the availability of the finest veterinary surgeons at the University of California at Davis saved Demon. The comments from the doctors attending him was that this boy was a lover, not a Demon.

CH. RINKY DINK'S SIR LANCELOT—"Lance"
Whelped: July 1972
Sire: Ch. Har-Dee's High Spirit
Dam: Ch. Rinky Dink's Robin
Breeder: Jean A. and William Petersen

Ch. Rinky Dink's Sir Lancelot

Lance is a dog every current breeder knows about. The sire of 134 champions, I first "came across" Lance one very hot day in 1975, at the Cocker Spaniel Club of New Jersey. Lance, as always, was being ably handled by Terry Stacy. Lance did not especially appreciate the heat and decided that this was not what he wanted to do. Needless to say he was not the variety winner that day. Two years later I judged the Futurity at the 1977 ASC show. I found among my Black winners the 9-12 male, Main-Dales Marathon Man, the 6-9 bitch, Rinky Dink's Smooth as Silk and the 9-12 bitch, Butch's Impish Delight—all sired by Lance. That was my first inkling of his potential as a sire. He certainly has realized that potential.

Lance was whelped in 1972, out of Ch. Rinky Dink's Robin and sired by Ch. Har-Dee's High Spirit. High Spirit is the sire of 17 champions while his sire, Ch. Lurola's Lookout, is the sire of 16 champions.

A beautiful black and tan dog with all-over balance and type and the merriest disposition ever, with his tail in constant motion, Lance finished his championship in short order, winning several sweepstakes. His first Best of Breed win was owner-handled by Jean Petersen at the Cocker Spaniel Club of the Midwest. Lance went on to Charlotte and Terry Stacy where, in limited showing, he won ten specialty Best of Breeds, several Group placements, and began his stud career in earnest.

His offspring are themselves beginning to be top producers. The Kaplar dogs and the winning records of such dogs as Peeping Tom will ensure a permanent place in history for one of the greatest producers of our time.

Ch. Camelot's Counterfeit

"Smash" was born in June 1984. Who knew at that time that this puppy would become such an integral and important part of Cocker Spaniel breed history?

Smash became a champion at just over 10 months of age. Along the way he won five large California Best In Sweepstakes, numerous sweepstakes varieties and Best Opposite Sex to Best In Sweepstakes. In his short campaign as a special he was awarded many Best of Variety wins. He was also awarded five Best of Breed awards at major specialty shows with entries in excess of 100 dogs. In addition to his Best of Breed wins, Smash also amassed several group placements at All-Breed events. He made several appearances at American Spaniel Club and was always in the final cuts in huge classes of specials.

One of Smash's last appearances was at Mission Valley CSC in 1994 at nearly ten years of age. He was awarded the Black BV from the Veteran's

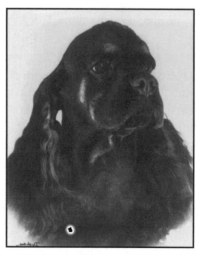

CH. CAMELOT'S COUNTERFEIT
Whelped: June, 1984
Breeder: Lou and Amy Weiss
Owner:Lou and Amy Weiss/Susan Burke

class and was also Best Veteran in Show. He made appearances at specialty shows in the Veteran and Producing Classes and in the Parade of Champions at nearly 13 years of age. Smash was always well received by ringside and was also voted as the number 3 favorite Black dog by the fancy (in a tie with one of his top winning sons) in a survey conducted by *The Cocker Spaniel Leader Magazine.*

Smash was bred by Lou and Amy Weiss and co-owned by his breeders and Susan Burke his entire life. Smash's accomplishments came to him solely due to his superior quality.

Ch. Empire's Brooklyn Dodger

Dodger has surpassed all others as a producer. The chances of another surpassing him are quite small as registrations in the breed has gone down.

Dodger has sired winners in all colors and has made the parti-color cocker the dominant variety in the breed. He passed away in March, 2000.

Top Producing Cocker of All Time
Ch. Empire's Brooklyn Dodger
Breeder: Jeff Wright

CHAPTER 13

Great Winning Dogs of the Recent Past

The Cocker Spaniels pictured in this chapter are some of America's top-winning male champions in the recent past.

Though unable to depict *every* top-winning male Cocker, this representative sampling of winning Cockers in all three Varieties portrays an image of some of the best that America had to offer during the last decade or so.

A top-winning dog of the 60's—Ch. Hi-Boots Such Brass

Ch. Camelot's Counterfeit
Whelped: June 20, 1984
Breeder: Louis M. and Amy Weiss
Owner: Susan Burke and Amy Weiss
Handlers: Bob and Jan Covey

"Smash's" show career started with a Reserve Winners Dog win from the 6-9 Puppy Dog class under a breeder/judge. He finished from the 9-12 Puppy Dog class with four majors, three large west coast Best in Sweepstakes, numerous Best Opposites to Best in Sweepstakes and numerous Sweepstakes Variety wins. He was nationally ranked in 1986 and in 1987.

Smash was a true "breeder's Cocker" with true breed type, elegance and the proper temperament so sought after.

Ch. Rendition Triple Play—"Andrew"
Sire:: Ch. Empire's Brooklyn Dodger
Dam: Ch. Derano's Desilu
Breeder: Brigitte Berg

Brigitte has had success with her Rendition line; most recently with Ch. Rendition Triple Play. Andrew's first big win was the ASC Futurity at 12 months of age and his first All Breed Best in Show with Jane Forsyth came at 15 months. One month later he won BOB at the ASC Summer National under Carl Liepman.

Andrew is Brigitte's first home-bred champion. He is producing consistently beautiful puppies that have been prominent in the last three ASC Nationals.

His greatest wins are numerous Best of Breeds including CSC of Arizona, Las Vegas, Orange County and Mission Valley.

Through his career, "Brogue" never failed to display his "show dog" attitude in the ring. He was retired early and finished his career with handler Bob Covey as the #1 Black and Tan in the nation and #3 all colors in 1978. Brogue continued to give his all from the veterans class (shown by his owner) and collected numerous BOV wins over top competition. His retirement from the veterans class ended with a Best Opposite Sex to Best of Variety win at the National Cocker Spaniel Specialty in Lincoln, Nebraska at 8½ years of age—and still flying around the ring!

Ch. Chess King's Board Boss
Whelped: October 13, 1975
Breeder: Billie and Chuck Ballantine
Owner: Billie Ballantine-Hayes
Handlers: Owner and Bob Covey

His greatest wins include 3 Group Firsts and numerous other placements. He won several Varieties at specialty shows.

However, his greatest fame came, not as a show dog, but as a producer of top show dogs. His get were top ASCOBs in '81, '82, '83 and '84. His daughter, Ch. Cottonwood's Colleen O'Brien was Best in Show at the January '82 ASC show, BOB at the July '82 ASC show and BOB at the January '83 ASC show. Another daughter, Ch. Makkell's Ziegfeld Girl was Best in Show at the January '84 ASC show.

Ch. Cottonwood's Congressman
Whelped: January 2, 1976
Breeder/Owner: Calvin E. Ward
Handler: Charles Self

Ch. Feinlyne By George
Whelped: August 15, 1976
Breeder/Owner: At and Annette Davies
Handlers: Al Davies and Mike Kinschsular

"George" attained his championship from the Bred By Exhibitor class. He is a multiple Best in Show, Group and Best of Breed winner.

George excelled in Cocker type and poise. Nothing rattled him. He has become one of the leading sires of the breed. He won Best of Varieties over the age of seven years. He was a source of pride and joy to his breeder/owners.

Ch. Frandee's Forgery
Whelped: December 7, 1981
Breeder: Karen Marquez
Owner: John and Dawn Zolezzi
Handler: Diana Kane

"Forgery's" greatest wins include Best in Show at the '87 ASC Annual Flushing Spaniel Specialty as well as numerous Bests of Breed and Group placements.

He was a short, hard back and shoulders that are well laid back. He had a strong rear with good length of leg. His coat was dense with proper texture. He had a very plush head with wide-set eyes and good expression. His showmanship was outstanding and he and Diana Kane made a superb team.

One of the top-winning dogs in American Spaniel Club history, "Brass" piled up numerous Best in Show and 17 Specialty Best of Breed wins. He won over 100 group placements including 38 Group Firsts. Brass' most memorable win was Best of Breed at the Cocker Spaniel Club of Las Vegas over 310 Cockers in competition.

He was balanced and sound with a lovely, refined head. He had clean shoulders with tremendous depth of forechest. His driving rear certainly called attention to his sloping, firm topline. He moved as he stacked—well-balanced and with a hard back. Best of all, he had a happy, typical Cocker temperament. He sired dozens of champions.

Ch. Frandee's Top Brass
Whelped: December 7, 1978
Breeder: Mr. and Mrs. Frank Wood
Owner/Handler: Bob and Jan Covey

"Mac" won his first major from the 6-9 Puppy Dog class and was Best in Sweepstakes that same day as well. He won another major from the 9-12 Puppy Dog class. He won numerous sweepstakes and was finished at 13 months of age. All of his wins are cherished by his breeder/owner but she has a special soft spot for his all-breed Bests in Show. He was ranked #1 Cocker for 1986.

Ch. Glen Arden's Real McCoy
Whelped: July 23, 1983
Breeder: Dorothy M. McCoy and
Arch T. McCoy
Owner: Dorothy McCoy
Handlers: Greg Anderson, Bob Covey and
Mike & Linda Pitts

Ch. Harrison's Peeping Tom
Whelped: February 1978
Breeder: Pauline Harrison
Owner: Mrs. Ronnie Muschal
Handler: Ted Young, Jr.

"Peeping Tom" had a sensational career which included 14 all-breed Bests in Show, 2 Specialty Bests of Breed, 54 Group Firsts and 58 other Sporting Group placements. In 1981, he was ranked the #1 Cocker Spaniel, was the nation's #1 Sporting Dog, was *Kennel Review's* Top Sporting Dog and was the winner of the Quaker Oats Award for most groups won in a year's time.

Ch. Homestead's Ragtime Cowboy
Whelped: September 24, 1978
Breeder/Owner: Bryan C. And
Marleen Rickertsen
Handlers: Owners, Charles Self and
Charles Nash

"Joe" has won multiple Bests in Sweepstakes, Bests of Breed, Bests in Show and was ranked #1 Parti-Color in '81 after having been shown only six months that year. He won Best in Futurity at the '79 Summer National and sired the '80 BOS to Best in Futurity and Best Parti-Color in Futurity at the '84 specialty.

Joe was well known for his true Cocker temperament, his style and showmanship in the ring. These characteristics are evident in his offspring.

"Floyd's" greatest win was his first Best in Show under Ted Young, Jr....the first Cocker Spaniel he had given the Best in Show award to. Floyd finished 1987 as the #2 Cocker in the nation.

Floyd was an outstanding showman gifted with an even temperament. He shows all out. He knows he's on display and makes the most of it. He was another in the line of great Hu-Mar champions and producers.

Ch. Hu-Mar's Good As Gold
Whelped: August 9, 1984
Breeder/Owner: Marilyn C. &
Hugh B. Spacht
Handler: Kyle Robinson

"Jarrett" was a multiple-group and specialty Best of Breed winner in both the United States and Canada.

His masculine head, smooth shoulders, short, hard back and driving rear are assets he passes on to his offspring. His children and grandchildren were group winners, Best of Breeds and even Best in Shows in the United States, Canada and South Africa. In 1982, Jarrett made the Top Ten Parti-Color as rated by *American Cocker Magazine* and #8 Parti-Color according to *Kennel Review's* system. Jarrett took his place at Jaywyck's as the # 1 stud dog and dabbled in obedience as well.

Can./Am. Ch. Jaywyck's The One 'N Only
Whelped: April 15, 1980
Breeder/Owner: Judith Wick Klepp
Handler: David L. Kittredge

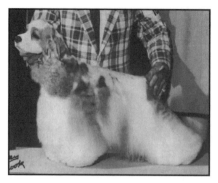

Ch. Juban's Georgia Jazz
Whelped: March 21, 1979
Breeder: Julian and Ann Smith
Owner: Charles and Jackie Rowe
Handier: Charles Rowe

"Jazz" completed his championship in four consecutive shows with four majors including the Summer National CSC Specialty, in July 1980. He has won numerous Bests of Variety at specialty shows and was a multiple Best of Breed winner at many large specialty shows. He had well over 20 Group placements. His greatest win was Best of Breed at the CSC of Southern California in '83. He was the # 1 Parti-Color in '83.

Jazz had probably one of the most elegant heads ever seen on a Cocker. He is well-balanced and moves effortlessly using his powerful rear correctly. Jazz was the model used by the artist who designed the AKC 100th Anniversary postage stamp. He was a joy to own and looks like he will be a top producer.

Ch. Kaplar's Jiminey Kricket
Whelped: September 9, 1984
Breeder: Robert & Ann Clement
Owner: Deryck & Christine Boutlier and
Laura Henson

"Jimmy" has many all-breed Bests in Show and Group placings as well as Bests of Breed at specialty shows. His greatest win was Best in Show at the American Spaniel Club in 1985.

Jimmy was well-balanced, beautifully headed and a strong moving dog with substance and a beautiful, correct coat.

"Beau" was ranked #4 Parti-Color in 1984. Among his most exciting wins was Best of Variety at the American Spaniel Club Futurity in 1983 and a Group First at the Richland County Kennel Club.

Beau's extreme type is the culmination of over 40 years of breeding Cocker Spaniels for the Duncans.

Ch. Laurim's Tri Performance
Whelped: January 1, 1982
Breeder/Owner/Handler: Dr. James R. And
Laurabeth Duncan

In "Ashe's" first year out as a special he won Best in Show at three all-breed shows. Other great wins include: Best Opposite Sex to Best of Breed at '83 ASC Summer Show, Best of Breed at Washington State CSC, Best Opposite Sex to Best of Breed at the Lincoln-Council Bluff Specialty. He also had numerous Group wins and Best of Variety wins.

Truly a "true" Sporting Dog.

Ch. Palm Hill's Mountain Ashe
Whelped: December 14, 1981
Breeder: deForest F. Jurkiewicz
Owner: Estate of Gladys W. Hoffman
Handler: Jerry Moon

Ch. Palm Hill Caro-Bu's Solid Gold
Whelped: October 25, 1981
Breeder: deForest Jurkiewicz and Carolyn
Emmerke
Owner: Hugh and Marilyn Spacht
Handlers: Charles Self and Greg Anderson

"Dreamer" had an exceptional show record in the short time he was campaigned. His happy-go-lucky spirit was passed on to his get as is evidenced by the fact that they, too, have had Group placings.

Dreamer has that "show ring" personality which made him very attractive to both the judges and the ringside. He has a great deal to offer to the Cocker fancy such as a beautiful head, correct topline and hard back. His get exhibited those same good features. A top producer as well.

Ch. Terje's Thunderbolt
Whelped: October 3, 1983
Breeder: Jeff Wright
Owner: Carol and Larry Dixon
Handlers: Linda Pitts

"Jack's" greatest wins include a Best in Show at Marion, Ohio; Bests of Breed at the Cocker Spaniel Club of Dallas and Cocker Spaniel Club of Chattanooga as well as numerous Group Firsts and placements throughout his year and a half specials career.

Jack culminated a lengthy search for a Parti-Color dog to special. Not only did he possess correct conformation and breed type, but was sound, open-marked, of stable temperament, had "attitude" galore and (above all) presented himself with true, correct, sporting dog movement.

"Illusion" is the Top Winning ABSCOB of 1999 and was BV at the ASC Show in 2000.

Ch. Bleumoon's Master of Illusions
Breeder: Michelle Mitchell

Hob Nobbins was a top winning parti-color in 1999.

Ch. JoBea's Hob Nobbins
Breeder: Henry & Bea Jones
Owner: Robert & Rita Lewis

CHAPTER 14

Great Winning Bitches of the Recent Past

The Cocker Spaniels pictured in this chapter are some of America's top-winning female champions in the recent past.

Though unable to depict *every* top-winning female Cocker, this representative sampling of winning Cockers in all three Varieties portrays an image of some of the best that America had to offer during the last decade or so.

A top-winning bitch of the 60's—Ch. Sagamore Toccoa.

Ch. Misty Wood JP TLC Miss Photogenic
Owner: Tracy Lynn Carroll

Misty was a BV from Open Class ASC, January 1999 and a multiple group winner.

Ch. Cherokee's Satin Doll
Owner: Brigitte Berg

Ch. Cherokee's Satin Doll is a top winner for Rendition Cockers.

Ch. DeRano's Desilu is a top winner and producer.

Ch. DeRano's Desilu
Owner: Brigitte Berg

"Annie" won a host of shows, including four Bests of Breed and one Best in Show at the American Spaniel Club. She also won an all-breed Best in Show, 18 Group Firsts and multiple Group placements.

With her faultless movement, beautiful conformation, showmanship plus, and big, dark eyes (designed to melt the hardest hearts), Annie won under the best of them. She was equally as special as a daily friend and companion. She proved herself as a producer as well.

Ch. Cottonwood's Colleen O'Brien
Whelped: October 8, 1978
Breeder: Mary Ann and George F. O'Brien
Owner: Judith Case
Handler: Don Johnston

Ch. Frandee's Celebration
Whelped: March 26, 1976
Breeder/Owner: Frank and Dee Dee Wood
Handler: Dee Dee Wood

"Celebration's" first big show win was a Best of Variety from the Open Class for a major over 5 specials. She went on to win a Group Fourth. She won the only Senior Futurity ever sponsored by the American Spaniel Club in July of '77. She was the top-winning Parti-Color in the nation in 1978.

She had four litters with a total of 14 puppies. Ten of her pups have become champions, with one son (Ch. Frandee's Footprint) becoming a Best in Show winner. She was a joy to own and to show! She was beautifully balanced and maintained condition easily. She was a terrific mother and a delightful house dog. What more could anyone ask or want?

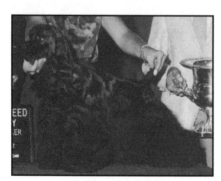

Ch. Kaplar's Kwik-Kopi
Whelped: April 8, 1981
Breeder/Owner: Harold & Laura Hensen
Handlers: Laura Henson and Greg Anderson

"Tracy" had many impressive wins but among her most memorable was Best of Variety at the American Spaniel Club National in 1983 and Best of Breed at the Council Bluffs-National week-end in 1984.

Tracy is the result of blending the Kaplar's two foundation lines of Artru and Royal Lancer stock. She was a compact bitch with a gorgeous front and rear, hard back, moving with tremendous reach and drive. She had a lovely coat, correct back coat, and a pretty head with a dark eye.

"Flo's" first big win was Best of Breed at the Connecticut-Westchester Cocker Spaniel Club in 1982. She went on to become the #1 ASCOB Cocker in 1983, was the #1 Cocker bitch (all varieties) the same year. She won seven all-breed Bests in Show, seven specialty Bests of Breed (including Best in Show at the '84 Flushing Spaniel Show), 20 Group Firsts and 52 other Group placements.

Flo was a beautiful bitch as well as a true sporting dog. She has a hard back, smooth neck and shoulders and correct reach. She and Ted were "poetry in motion." Flo combined energy, grace and stamina when she moved. Weather was no deterrent to her willingness to put on a good show—she moved well in extreme heat or in rain.

Ch. Makkell's Ziegfeld Girl
Whelped: August 24, 1980
Breeder: Marilyn A. Fink
Owner: Muriel and Ken Kellerhouse
Handler: Ted Young, Jr.

"Missy's" show career was spectacular. Her first "big" win as a special was to go Best of Breed at the Cocker Spaniel Club of Kentucky. For the next three years she accrued 81 Bests of Variety, 12 Group Firsts and three Bests in Show as well as many Group placements.

She thrived on the show ring and the applause. She was a once-in-a-lifetime thrill that breeders hope and pray for but seldom see. She was the Russ' bitch on paper but she belonged to all the Cocker fancy in their hearts.

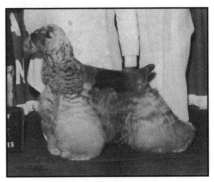

Ch. Russ' Winter Beauty
Whelped: October 1974
Breeder/Owner: Larry and Norma Russ
Handler: Don Johnston

Ch. Shardeloe's Selena
Whelped: July 1970
Breeder: Mrs. Fred Hicks-Beach
Owner: Dr. & Mrs. Clarence Smith
Heyday Kennels, Reg.
Handlers: Terry and Charlotte Stacy

"Selena's" show record included 17 Bests in Show, 86 Group Firsts, 166 other Group placings, 18 Bests of Breed at specialty shows. She was Best of Breed at the '73 and '74 American Spaniel Club's shows and Best of Variety from '72 through '75 at the ASC. She was the top-winning Cocker for '73 and '74 and one of the nation's top Sporting Dogs.

Although her first litters were not whelped until she was five, her qualities as a producer were reflected in nine champions and she is the granddam of 51 champions. She was one in a million.

Ch. Showtime Classy Cheerleader
Whelped: January 1, 1985
Breeder/Owner: Donald B. And
Carol Ann Harris
Handlers: Bob & Jan Covey

"Cheer" finished at 9 months and 26 days of age. She won the '86 American Spaniel Club National Futurity. She was ranked #2 overall top-winning bitch for '86, and she was the #5 ASCOB overall.

Some of her greatest wins include winning the Variety Sweepstakes at five different specialties and winning Best in Sweepstakes at three specialties.

"Termite" is the only obedience-titled dog to win a Best in Show at the American Spaniel Club! In all, she won 16 all-breed Bests in Show, 19 Bests of Breed, 50 Group Firsts, 63 other Group placements, and 173 Bests of Variety. In 1981, she came out of retirement to win Best of Breed at the Washington State Cocker Spaniel Club specialty at almost eight years of age!

"Termite" excelled in everything she attempted—as a conformation dog, as an obedience dog and as a brood bitch. One of her sons is a Best in Show dog and two of her daughters are High in Trial winners.

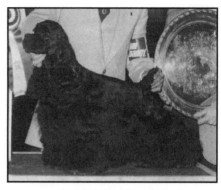

Can./Am. Ch. Tabaka's Tidbit O'Wynden, CDX
Whelped: July 24, 1973
Breeder: Dennis J. and Wynn N. Bloch
Owner: Ruth N. Tabaka
Handlers: Jim Hall, Bill Ernst, Ted Young, Jr.

Beauty was one of the top winning ASCOB's in the country in 1999 and continues her winning record with numerous groups.

Ch. Showtime Coronation Beauty
Sire: Ch. Fanny Hill Hi Plains Drifter
Dam: Ch. Toccata's Black Attraction
Breeder: Don & Carol Harris
Owners: Barry & Sherry Blondheim
Handler: Don Rodgers

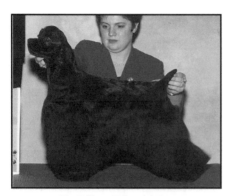

Ch. Gallant Colorado's Best
Owner: Nancy Gallant

Ch. Gallant Colorado's Best was the top winning black bitch for 1999. She was BOS to BV at the 2000 ASC Show.

CHAPTER 15

Top Producing Dogs

1. Ch. Empire's Brooklyn Dodger   152
2. Ch. Rinky Dink's Sir Lancelot   134
3. Ch. Scioto Bluff's Sinbad   118
4. Ch. Dreamridge Dominoe   108
5. Ch. Palm Hill Caro Bu's Solid Gold   106
6. Ch. Orient's It's a Pleasure   103
7. Ch. Hu-Mar's Go For The Gold, CD   93
8. Ch. Artru Skyjack   84
9. Ch. Windy Hill's 'Tis Demi's Demon   82
10. Ch. Stockdale Town Talk   80

Am. Can. Ch. Eng. Sh. Champion Piperhill's King Arthur*

*Top Cocker Sire in England

Ch. Empire's Brooklyn Dodger

Ch. Rinky Dink's Sir Lancelot

Ch. Scioto Bluff's Sinbad

Ch. Dreamridge Dominoe

Ch. Palm Hill Caro Bu's Solid Gold

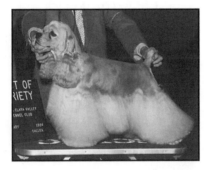

Ch. Orient's a Pleasure

Ch. Hu-Mar's Go For The Gold, CD

Ch. Artru Skyjack

Ch. Windy Hill's 'Tis Demi's Demon

Ch. Stockdale Town Talk

Am. Can. Ch. Eng. Sh. Champion Piperhill's King Arthur

Arthur, another of the great Ch Palm Hill's Krugerand sons by Ch Bobwins Special Blend, the dam of eleven Champions herself. He was bred by Don and Sydney Johnson (Piperhill) and sold to Bill and Cindy Mixon (Denali Cockers), and now owned by Mrs Yvonne Knapper (Sundust) in England. In limited breedings this dog has stamped his heritage well. His offspring and their get continue to produce Champions that dominate the rings wherever they are shown.

Am. Can. Ch. Eng. Sh. Champion
Piperhill's King Arthur
Top Winner —England & USA
Top Producer—USA
Top Producing American Cocker All
Time—England

His record speaks for itself as well: Eleven AKC Champions, Ten English Champions, One IABCA International Champion, and four Canadian Champions with more on their way to their titles in England. In the conformation ring he was extremely competitive showing eleven times only as a Special in the USA with 9 BOV and 2 group 4s, and I group 2, retiring in the number two spot USA before going to England where he still has them shaking their heads. His English record consists of 26

Championship Certificates and a Reserve BIS at the Gun Dog Society of Wales (entry of close to 9000). Shown twice at Crufts, he won the CC the first time and came back at 11½ years old to win the Veterans class stripped down in 1999. He is the producer of the first Full Gun Dog Champion in over thirty years and also many CC winners as well as Reserve BIS. Yvonne Knapper says that " He is without a doubt the best Stud Dog ever at Sundust, and truly a gentleman at home", quite a compliment from England's top breeder.

Arthur now has three generations of top winners including Best In Show being actively shown in Canada, England and the USA. His influence promises to make him truly one of the great American Cockers in the history books.

CHAPTER 16

Top Producing Bitches

1.	Ch. Saratoga's Secret Center	25
2.	Ch. Kamps' Kountry Kiss	23
3.	Ch. Laurim's Star Performance	20
4.	Ch. Kaplar's Kolleen	18
4.	Ch. Tamara's All That Glitters	18
5.	Ch. Palm Hill's Starlet O'Hara	17
6.	Ch. Grisard Gymnastic Gold	16
6.	Ch. Waltann's Show N Tell	16
7.	Ch. Seenar's Seductress	15
7.	Ch. Tri Pod's Firefly	15
7.	Ch. Wendadam's White Shoulders	15
8.	Ch. Artru Delightful II	14
8.	Ch. Frandee's Susan	14
8.	Int. Ch. Honey Creek Vivacious	14
8.	Ch. Low Desert Thanks A Million	14
8.	Ch. Windy Hill 'Tis Lipton's Rebuff	14
9.	Ch. Canyon Convicted of Forgery	13
9.	Ch. Cobb's Kathleen	13
9.	Ch. Lydgate's Golden Girl	13
9.	Ch. Marquis Mistletoe	13
9.	Ch. Shalimar's Soft Touch	13
10.	Ch. Sharob's Emerald Image	12

Ch. Saratoga's Secret Center

Ch. Kamps' Kountry Kiss

Ch. Laurim's Star Performance

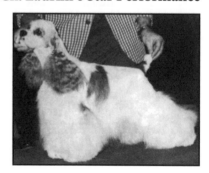

Ch. Tamara All That Glitters

Ch. Seenar's Seductress

Ch. Tri Pod's Firefly

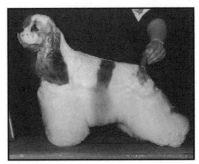

Ch. Artru Delightful II

Ch. Frandee's Susan

Int. Ch. Honey Creek Vivacious

Ch. Low Desert Thanks A Million

Ch. Canyon Convicted of Forgery

Ch. Cobb's Kathleen

Ch. Lydgate's Golden Girl

Ch. Marquis Mistletoe

Ch. Shalimar's Soft Touch

CHAPTER 17

How The Dog Show Game Works

The backbone of the dog show is the individual, the all-breed and specialty dog clubs. By joining a dog club you begin to learn the ins and outs of raising and showing dogs. Boy, is there a lot of information waiting for you out there! Getting that information can sometimes be difficult. By reading this book you have shown you are interested enough to get going on your own.

Most dog clubs have educational meetings where you can learn interesting facts about the sport. The best entry point is a specialty club, that is, a club dealing with a single breed. For instance, The American Spaniel Club is the "parent club" for Cocker Spaniels. If you are not a member, find the club nearest to you and inquire about joining.

Specialty clubs are the best place to learn about your breed. Their major goal is to educate their membership and to hold American Kennel Club (AKC) licensed shows. Specialty clubs are under the overall "jurisdiction" of their (parent) national club. However, in order to hold a dog show, they must be given approval by the AKC and hold the show under AKC rules. The club picks their own judges from a list of AKC-licensed judges.

It's apparent that the AKC is a pretty important organization, so let's talk about it before we go on to describing dog shows themselves.

The AKC is a private organization, not a government entity as is the case in many countries. The club is run by delegates who are elected by their local clubs. The local clubs in turn, are member clubs of the AKC. The delegates elect a Board of Directors from their own ranks. The Board is entrusted with formulating policy and direction for the club. The Board hires the President and he acts as its Chief Executive Officer. The AKC is over a 20 million dollar corporation and is located at 260 Madison Ave, New York, New York 10016. It is chartered in that state. The AKC only rarely puts on shows of its own. The major functions of AKC are:

- Registration of pure bred dogs

- Publication of a stud register

- Keeping and publishing statistics through the *AKC Gazette*, its monthly publication

- Recognizing new dog clubs as show giving entities under AKC development rules

- Education of the public through publications, seminars, and audio/visual media

- Sponsorship of research into major medical/physical problems of dogs

- Sanctioning of dates and places for dog clubs to hold their shows

- Licensing of judges to officiate at AKC licensed events

- Providing oversight of the shows themselves through AKC field representatives

- U.S. representative to international bodies interested in promoting the sport of pure bred dogs

Now, let's tackle the concept of dog shows themselves. Naturally, enough of you would like to participate. In order to do this you must have a purebred dog. By "purebred," it is meant that your dog must be eligible for registration by AKC. You will recall when you bought your puppy you were given registration papers. If you have not filled them out yet, do so now. Until your dog is registered with the AKC and gets an individual registration number, you can't show him. Once you have that magic piece of paper in your hands you can enter dog shows to your heart's delight. Of course, each entry fee will cost you a sum of money. The going rate today is about $20.00.

OK, now we get into it. Your local specialty club is going to hold a show and they are encouraging you to enter. So, nothing ventured, nothing gained. The show chairman makes sure you get an entry form and even waits around for you to fill it out. You need to put down your dog's registered name and number, his birthdate, his parents' names, who were the breeders (it's all on the registration form) and your name as owner. That's it—except for the check in the proper amount. Oh yes, you must select the class he will be in. Now what do we mean by class? Dog shows, like most sporting events, have various classifications—some by age and others by the amount of winning the dog has done. Let's take a look at the various classes offered and find out who is eligible for them.

The classes include:

- **Puppy**
  Over 6 months & under 9 months

- **Puppy**
  Over 9 months & under 12 months

- **Novice**
  Has not yet won a blue ribbon in adult classes, three first prizes in the Novice class, or one or more championship points prior to close of entry

- **Bred by Exhibitor**
  Exhibited by the Breeder of Record (you must have bred and currently own the dog to show in this class)

- **American Bred**
  Must have been bred in America

- **Open Class**
  Open to all, including puppies

- **Best of Breed**
  AKC Champions only in this class

In certain specialty shows, there may be a class for 12-18 month old puppies.

Once entered, you need to make sure your dog is ready to be shown. If you have not learned to trim your dog, now is not the time to start practicing! Either take him back to the breeder or to a professional trimmer, one who knows about cockers. Observe them carefully; it's a good idea to learn to trim your own dog. Otherwise, it gets expensive. Consult the chapter, "The Versatile Cocker As A Show Dog," to get a good idea what trimming is all about. That same chapter has very useful directions on training your dog for the show ring.

The dog show itself is a novel experience for the uninitiated. Sights and sounds like you've never seen or heard before. It's a good idea to latch onto a more experienced exhibitor to go with you the first time. Find your ring and be sure you carefully observe the time schedule, which you received from the show superintendent the week preceding the show. If you were lucky, there were even directions on how to get to the show site.

Since the dog show world still seems to cling to its male chauvinistic ways, dogs are shown first, followed by bitches. The procedure is to start off with the youngest age puppy classes and work their way through all the classes for males. (The classes are just like those listed above.) Once the judge has selected a winner for each of the classes, he brings back all the class winners to be compared against each other and the breed standard. Yes, there is a specific blueprint laid down by each breed's parent club and accepted by the American Kennel Club as to what each breed should look like. (Refer to the chapter on the standard for more in-depth information.) The judge's purpose in comparing all his male winners is to select the one closest to the standard to award AKC points toward his championship. The number of points for each breed is determined by the number competing on that day, in that geographic location. Look in front of a show catalog and you will find a schedule of points. It's different for each breed and each area of the country. It depends on the popularity of the breed and how many dogs were shown in this area last year. It's an intricate formula; all worked out by the statisticians of AKC.

To become a champion, your dog needs to earn 15 championship points, including two major wins. The major wins must be earned under two different judges and your dog cannot finish his championship without winning under a minimum of three different judges. A major win consists of 3, 4, or 5 points. The more dogs competing, the greater number of points awarded. Five is the maximum at any one show, no matter how many dogs are defeated.

After all the males have been shown, the judge repeats the same procedure when judging the bitches. After he has selected his point-winning bitch, the winners dog and the winners bitch come into the ring with the champions competing in the Best of Breed ("Specials") class to compete for Best of Breed or Best of Variety.

In Cocker Spaniels, there are three Varieties: There is the Black Variety (which includes blacks and black and tans competing); the ASCOB Variety (which means Any Solid Color Other than Black to include buffs, chocolates, and chocolate and tans). The third Variety is the Parti-Color, (which include red and whites, black and whites, and tri-colors—which are black and whites with the tan markings of the black and tan added), and roans (which are fairly rare in American Cocker Spaniels). Sidle over to the English Cocker ring if you want to see a good roan pattern.

Since this is an all-breed show and all 140+ AKC-approved breeds can be shown, there is no Best of Breed Cocker award given. The judge selects only a Best of Variety, a Best of Winners (that means either the dog or bitch is selected as the best of the winners of the day), and a Best of Opposite Sex to Best of Variety. That means that if a male Champion won Best of Variety, then the judge would pick a bitch to be the best of her sex. It can happen the other way around, too. The judge, if he sees fit, does not have to pick a champion for these top awards. The Winners Dog and Winners Bitch can be selected to be Best of Variety and/or Best of Opposite Sex. Each of the variety winners go on to compete in the sporting group against the 24 other breed winners that make up its group. Before this gets too complicated, please refer to Figure 53 which shows the classes and the winning progression at an all-breed dog show. In a way, it's like a basketball tournament. The seven groups make up the brackets and they move along until there are only seven finalists left. Then the judge makes the ultimate award of Best in Show. One last point, if the Best of Winners dog or bitch had earned fewer points by winning its portion of the competition than the animal it defeated, it will gain the greater number of points; i.e., the Winners Bitch won two points but the Winners Dog won five. By going Best of Winners, the bitch would pick up the three additional points awarded the dog and gain a major. The dog would still have his five points so the net effect would be that both took home five-point major wins.

All-breed shows are the most prevalent in this country. But, there is another type of show that is designed specifically for a single breed. It's called a Specialty Show. Any breed club that is recognized and licensed by the AKC may hold one. As a result there are hundreds of these shows held

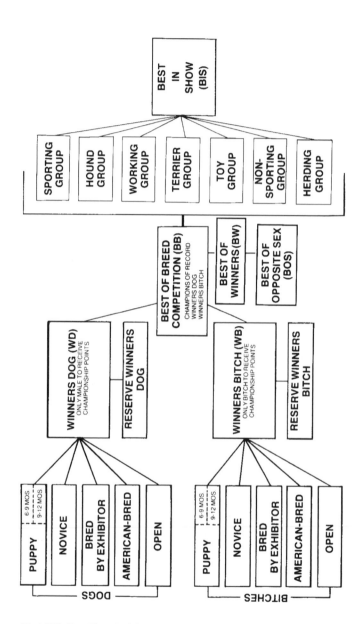

Figuere 53. AKC's Dog Show Judging Progression

every year. The difference between a specialty show and an all-breed show is that the three variety winners compete directly for the coveted Best of Breed award. There is also a Best of Opposite Sex award. These are considered very important wins. AKC championship points are also awarded at these shows.

A third type of show—and one that seems to be the kind of event for novice and expert alike—is the Sanctioned Match. Again, most of these are held under AKC sanction but no championship points are awarded. It's a practice ground. New owners can show their own dogs and make all the first-timer mistakes without penalty or embarrassment. Experienced breeders use it as a training ground for their newest show prospects. The judges are usually professional handlers or breeders who want to qualify to become regular judges. It's fun and a great learning experience. There are both all-breed and specialty sanctioned matches. Check with your local dog club for information on these events.

On several occasions, reference has been made to "the judge" who selects the winning dogs. These ladies and gentlemen are duly approved by the American Kennel Club. They are usually persons who have been successful breeders or professional handlers of many years' standing. They have filled out arduous questionnaires about their involvement in dogs, taken tests on the breeds they wish to judge, and have been interviewed by an AKC Field Representative. Once they have passed these "hurdles," their names are published in the *American Kennel Gazette*, the monthly magazine of the AKC. Persons having knowledge of these candidates may write to the AKC either for, or against, them. The final step is a review and analysis by an AKC panel. Using prescribed guidelines, they grant a candidate one or more breeds. The candidate must go through similar subsequent applications in order to judge additional breeds.

Once granted his or her initial set of breeds, the fledgling judge must judge all of these breeds on five occasions to be eligible to apply for others. During this period, the judge is known as a "provisional judge." Their actions are carefully watched by an AKC Field Representative and a report is given on their ring procedure and general knowledge. Even after being granted status as a regular judge, all judges are periodically evaluated and a report submitted to the judge and to AKC.

At this point, I must warn you about a terribly infectious disease you could pick up by attending your first dog show. It's called the "BUG" and people who catch it can become dog show bugs for the rest of their lives.

Their friends think they are off their rocker since they suddenly start talking about "bitches" and "points" and other stuff that makes no sense to normal people. Dog show bugs often give up golf and on weekends can be found out in the sun in the middle of a ring howling about what a great win they just pulled off. Have pity on them, but beware—it could happen to YOU!

To learn more about the breed, I suggest you subscribe to the Cocker Spaniel magazine:

The Cocker Spaniel Leader
Shirley Estel, Editor
9700 Jersey Mill Road, N.W.
Pataskala, Ohio 43062
$40 per year, third class postage rate
$50 per year, first class postage rate

Bibliography

Periodicals

Allen, Michael (ed.), *American Cocker Magazine*, numerous articles from several issues.

Ardnt, TK., "Breeders Forum." *Akita World*, December 1985.

Asseltyne, Claire, "Form Follows Function," *The Great Dane Reporter*, May-June, July-August, September-October 1980.

Bierman, Ann, "Feeding Your Puppy," *The Golden Retriever Review*, March 1987.

Brown, Russell V, "Nutrition and Feeding of the Basenji," *The Basenji*, Feb. 1987.

Burnham, Patricia Gail, "Breeding, Litter Size and Gender," *American Cocker Review*, 1981.

Donnely, Mary, "Caesarian Section...The Home Care," *Min Pin Monthly*, March 1987.

Furumoto, Howard H., "Frozen and Extended Semen," *The ILIO, Hawaii's Dog News*, Oct. & Nov. 1986.

Grossman, Alvin, "The Basis of Heredity," *American Kennel Club Gazette*, April 1980.

Grossman, Alvin, "Color Inheritance," *The American Cocker Review*, March, April, May and June 1974.

Grossman, Alvin, "Faults and Double Faults," *The American Cocker Review*, March 1980.

Grossman, Marge, "Evolution of the Cocker Head," *The American Cocker Review*, June 1961.

Grossman, Marge, "To the Victors," *The American Cocker Review*, August 1966.

Hane, Curtis B., "Training Your Dog, A Consumers Guide," *The Great Dane Reporter*, March-April 1987.

Mohrman, R.K., "Supplementation—May Be Hazardous To Your Pet's Health," *The Great Dane Reporter*, March-April 1980.

Schaeffer, Ruth C., "The View From Here, A Breeder's Report On Collecting Frozen Sperm," *American Kennel Club Gazette*, November 1982.

Wittels, Bruce R., "Nutrition of Newly Born and Growing Individuals," *The Great Dane Reporter*, January/February 1985.

Books

Austin, Norman A. & Austin, Jean S., *The Complete American Cocker Spaniel*, New York: Howell Book House, 1993.

Bailey, Joan, *How to Help Gun Dogs Train Themselves*, Swan Valley Press, Hillsboro, OR, 1993.

Benjamin, Carol L., *Mother Knows Best, The Natural Way to Train Your Dog*. New York: Howell Book House, 253 pgs., 1987.

Burnham, Patricia G., *Play Training Your Dog*. New York: St. Martin's Press, 1980.

Burns, Marsh A. & Fraser, Margaret N., *The Genetics of the Dog*. Farnham Royal Eng.: Commonwealth Agricultural Bureau, 1952.

Connett, Eugene V, *American Sporting Dogs*. D. Van Nostrand Co., Inc.

Craig, Ralph, *Elementary Spaniel Field Training*. New York: American Spaniel Club, 21 pgs, 1947.

Evans, Job M., *The Evans Guide For Counseling Dog Owners*. New York: Howell Book House, Inc., 1985.

Gaines Dog Research Center, *Training The Hunting Dog*. General Foods Corporation, 15 pgs, 1973.

Greer, Frances, Editor, *A Century of Spaniels*; *Vols. I & II*. Amherst, Massachusetts: American Spaniel Club, 1980.

Grossman, Alvin & Grossman, Beverly, *Winning with Pure-Bred Dogs*, Wilsonville, OR: Doral Publishing, 1991.

Hutt, Fredrick B., *Genetics For Dog Breeders*. San Francisco: W.H. Freeman & Co., 245 pgs, 1979.

Little, C.C., *The Inheritance of Coat Color In Dogs*. New York: Howell Book House, Inc., 194 pgs, 1973.

McDowell, Lyon, *The Dog in Action*, New York: Howell Book House, Inc. 1974.

Moffit, Ella B., *The Cocker Spaniel: Companion, Shooting Dog and Show Dog*. New York: Orange Judd Publishing Company, 335 pgs, 1949.

Sabella, Frank & Kalstone, Shirlee, *The Art of Handling Show Dogs*. Hollywood: B & E Publications, 140 pgs, 1980.

Smith, Anthony, *The Human Pedigree*. Philadelphia: J.B. Lippincott Company, 308 pgs, 1975.

Whitney, Leon F., D.V.M., *How to Breed Dogs*. New York: Orange Judd Company, 1947.

Whitney, Leon F., D.VM., *This is the Cocker Spaniel*. New York, Orange Judd Company, 1947.

Winge, Dr. Ojvind, *Inheritance in Dogs*. Comstock Publishing Company, Ithaca, New York: 1950.

INDEX

A

Ch. Adam's Black Perfection 160
Adams, Mr. & Mrs. S. T. 183
Afghan Hound 39
Airedale Terrier 157
Allen, Michael. 241
American Cocker Magazine 207, 241
American Cocker Review 29, 30, 165, 185,
    194, 241
American Kennel Club (AKC) 3, 5, 8, 12,
    15-16, 22, 29, 92, 121, 125, 127-128, 145,
    150, 153, 175, 208, 233-239
American Kennel Gazette 239
American Spaniel Club. 11-18, 20, 29, 129,
    139, 142, 143-148, 150, 172, 178, 199
Anderson, Carl & Rosalie 31
Anderson, Gregg 118, 169, 205, 216
Anselmi, Edna 31, 166, 195
Argyll *(prefix)* 181
Ch. Argyll's Archer 181, 182
Ch. Argyll's Enchantress 181
Artru *(prefix)* 23, 163, 164, 165, 169, 172,
    191, 216
Ch. Artru Action 191, 192
Ch. Artru Adventure 164
Ch. Artru Ambassador 163
Artru Available 163
Ch. Artru Crackerjack 164
Artru Delightful II 165, 214, 227, 230
Ch. Artru Hot Rod 164
Ch. Artru Johnny Be Good . 164, 187, 191, 192
Ch. Artru Red Baron 164, 191, 193
Artru Remarkable 163
Ch. Artru Sandpiper 164, 191, 192
Ch. Artru Skyjack 164, 165, 191, 221, 224
Ch. Artru Slick Chick 164
Ch. Artru Trinket 191
Ashley's Cherry Jubilee 195
Audacious Lady 160, 183
Aurelius, Marcus 195
Austin, Norman 10, 30, 163, 169, 185, 188, 242

B

Ballantine, Chuck & Billie 203
Ch. Bar-C-Kar's Peau Rouge 192
Bartelme, Heather 140
Basset Hound 37
Beach, Mrs. Fred Hicks 218
BeGay Kennels 56
Ch. Benbow's Tanbark. 186
Benhoff, Art & Ruth 23, 30, 163-165,
    191, 193
Berg, Brigitte. 172
Berol, Henry 143-145
F.T Ch. Berol Lodge Glen Garry 145
Blackstone *(prefix)* 23, 24, 27, 177
Blackstone Chief. 27
Ch. Blackstone Reflector 24
Blair, Mrs. Shiras 162
Blake, Mr. Dennis. 149
Ch. Bleumoon's Master of Illusions 211
Bloch, Dennis J. & Wynn N 219
Ch. Bobwin's Boy Eagle 167
Ch. Bobwin's Sir Ashley 47, 172, 195
Borzoi 39
Bostick, Mr. & Mrs. Hagood 27
Boston Terrier 43
Boutilier, Deryck & Christine 169
Breed Standard 32, 34, 41-46, 236
    Coat. 44
    Coloring 44
    Disqualifications. 46
    Gait 45
    Proportion 42
    Size. 41
    Temperament. 46
Breeders, Breeding. 47, 48, 49, 56, 76, 86,
    92, 157
Breeding Better Cocker Spaniels 61
Ch. Brightfield Delight. 178
Brister, Mrs. Mildred 20
Brower, Ivan. 146
Brown, Mr. & Mrs. Fred. 20
Ch. Bubble Up of Stockdale 159
Buck, Leonard 20, 23, 24, 176, 177

Burke, Susan 198, 199
Burns, W. Chalmers 146
Butch's Impish Delight 197
Buxton, Ron 168

C

Callahan, Clint 161
Camby *(prefix)* 30
Camelot *(prefix)* 31
Ch. Camelot's Confetti 119
Ch. Camelot's Counterfeit 198, 202
Ch. Camelot's Court Jester 119
Ch. Camelot's Cupcake, CD 120
Camelot's Second Hand Rose, TD 126
Camino's Cheetah 145
FT Ch. Camino's Red Rocket 146
Ch. Canyon Convicted of Forgery . . . 227, 231
Ch. Carcyn's Chula Vista, WDX 142
Carlen's *(prefix)* 196
Ch. Carmor's Rise and Shine 18, 19, 31, 159, 185
Carro *(prefix)* 31
Ch. Carronade Trigger 82
Case, Judith 215
Cassilis *(prefix)* 22
Championships, American 233-240
Charlie's Ebony Angel, UD 140
Ch. Charmary Consomme, CDX/TD 123
Ch. Cherokee's Satin Doll 214
Ch. Chess King's Board Boss 203
Chidal's Licorice Kiss, CD 137
Ch. Chidal's Licorice Prince, CDX 137
Chidal's Something Special, CDX 124, 137
Churchman, Mrs. W.M. 22
Ch. Clarkdale Calcutta 195
Ch. Clarkdale Capital Stock 188
Claythorne *(prefix)* 27
Clement, Robert & Ann 208
Coat Color 44-45, 47-89
  Bi-Color 73-77
  Black 44, 47-51
  Buff 51-56
  Chocolate/Liver 56-72
  Mismarks 87-89
  Parti-Color 44, 77-82
  Tri-Color 82-87
Cobb, Bain 24, 176
Cobb, Mr. & Mrs. R. Kenneth 20, 25, 178, 180, 181, 185, 186
Cobb, Mrs. R. K 20
Ch. Cobb's Kathleen 227, 231
Cocker Hall of Fame 30
Cockers Calling 166, 188

Cocker Spaniel Breeder's Club of
  New England 19
Cocker Spaniel Club of Kentucky 19
The Cocker Spaniel Leader 240, 199
Ch. Coldstream Guard of Cordova 23, 24
Collie 157
Ch. Cordova Coccade 23
Ch. Cordova Cordial 23
Cordova *(prefix)* 23
Ch. Cottonwood's Colleen O'Brien . . 203, 215
Ch. Cottonwood's Congressman 203
Covey, Bob & Jan 169, 202-203, 205, 218
Covey, Byron & Cameron 30
Crabbe, Mr. & Mrs. Joseph 27
Craig, Ralph 141, 142
Creekwood Miss Showoff 194
Creighton, Sherry 149

D

Ch. Dabar Agitator, UD/TD 123, 125, 137
Ch. Dau-Han Dan Morgan 195
Dautel 27
Davies, Al & Annette 169, 204
Deidree Shannon Dodge, CDX/WD . . 123-124
Ch. DeKarlos Dashaway 188
Ch. DeKarlos Day Dreams 185
Denlinger Publishers, Ltd. 10, 61
Ch. Denzil's Super Daddy 169
Ch. DeRano's Desilu 215
Diamond's Jacobus Jonker, CD 149
Disqualifications, standard 46
Dixon, Larry & Carol 210
Dodge, Debbie 123, 124
Dodson, Dr. J. Eugene 145
Dodsworth, Miss Alice 19, 20, 23, 175
Dominguez, Carlos & Cynthia 142
Doty, Mari 29, 30, 116, 166, 169
Doty, Norman & Mari 30
Doyle, Liz 123, 125, 137
Dreamridge *(prefix)* 30, 195
Ch. Dreamridge Dinner Date 30, 194, 195
Ch. Dreamridge Dominoe 30, 173, 194, 221, 223
Ch. Dunbar 20
Duncan, Dr. James R. & Laurabeth 209
Dur-Bet *(prefix)* 170, 171, 172
Ch. Dur-Bet's Knight To Remember . . 171, 172
Ch. Dur-Bet's Kristmas Knight 171
Ch. Dur-Bet's Leading Lady 171
Ch. Dur-Bet's Nightie Night 172
Ch. Dur-Bet's Pick The Tiger, CD 172, 196
Dur-Bet's Scandal Sheet 171
Ch. Dur-Bet's Tantalizer 171, 172
Ch. Dur-Bet's Tiger Paws 172

E

Easdale *(prefix)* 27
Elder, H. Stewart & Mary 188
Ch. Elder's So Lovely 189
Elderwood Bangaway 188, 189
Emmerke, Carolyn 210
Ch. Empire's Brooklyn Dodger . . 199, 221, 222
English Cocker Spaniel . . 3, 7, 25, 78, 147, 149,
153, 154
Ernst, Bill & Gay 56, 169, 219
Ch. Essanar East Side 169
Evans, Job Michael 133

F

Fabis, Ron 30, 190, 194, 195
Ch. Feinlyne By George 204
Fink, Marilyn A. 217
Flirtation Walk 171
Ch. Found 20, 23
Fox, Dr. Michael W. 133
Fraclin *(prefix)* 190
Ch. Frandee's Celebration 216
Ch. Frandee's Footprint 216
Ch. Frandee's Forgery 169, 204
Ch. Frandee's Susan 227, 230
Ch. Frandee's Top Brass 205
Funk, Dick 186
Futurity 15, 167, 172, 197, 202, 206, 209,
216, 216

G

Gable, Clark 146
Gait 45
Ch. Gallant Colorado's Best 220
General appearance 41-46
German Shepherd Dog 177
Gilmans, O.B. 20
Ch. Glen Arden's Real McCoy 205
Ch. Glenmurray's Tally Ho, CDX 137
Glidmere Buzz 178
Godfrey, Tom 180, 181
Gorr, Liz 195
Ch. Gravel Hill Gold Opportunity 164
Great Dane 129
Greer, Frances 9, 139
Griffin, Kenna 139
Ch. Grisard Gymnastic Gold 227

H

Ch. Hadley's Trumpeter 163
Hall, Jim & Beth 31, 190, 219
Hall-Way *(prefix)* 190
Ch. Hall-Way Hoot Mon 173, 190, 194

Hamsher, Bud & Ida 30
Hane, Curtis B. 129
Hansen, Elaine 137
Ch. Har-Dee's High Spirit 197
Harrington, Charles & Donna Martin 197
Harris, Donald B. & Carol Ann 219
Harrison, Pauline 206
Ch. Harrison's Peeping Tom 206
Haywood, Myrtle 186
Head, J. Stanley 145
Health Registry 17, 29
Henson, Harold ("Kap") & Laura . . 31, 208, 216
Hereditary & Congenital Defects
Committee 30
Heyday *(prefix)* 218
Hi-Boots *(prefix)* 185
Ch. Hi-Boots Such Brass 73, 185, 201
Hilder, Carol 196
Hip Dysplasia (HD) 29
Ch. Hob-Nob-Hill's Tribute 172, 196
Hodges, Andrew 27
Ch. Hollyrock Harvester 171
Holmeric Kennels 25
Ch. Holmeric of Brookville 25, 26
Ch. Homestead's Ragtime Cowboy 206
Homozygous 55, 86
Honey Creek *(prefix)* 30, 77, 161, 163, 190
Ch. Honey Creek Cricket 161
Honey Creek Freckles 163
Ch. Honey Creek Halo 162, 163
Ch. Honey Creek Harmonizer . . . 162, 163, 190
Ch. Honey Creek Havana 190
Ch. Honey Creek Heir 162
Ch. Honey Creek Heirloom 161, 162
Ch. Honey Creek Hero 161
Ch. Honey Creek Vivacious 161, 162, 190,
227, 230
Huff, Lori J.R 137
Ch. Hu-Mar's Good As Gold 207
Ch. Hu-Mar's Go For The Gold 221, 224
Hutchinson, William 141

I

Ch. Idahurst Belle II 20, 21
Isola, Shirley 122

J

Jackson Memorial Laboratory 78
Ch. Jaywyck's The One 'N Only 207
Jet Job's Jolly Rajah, CDX 137
Jim Crow's Glow 22
Ch. Jo-Be-Glen's Bronze Falcon 191, 193
Jo-Be-Glen's Honeycomb 192, 193
Ch. JoBea's Hob Nobbins 211

Johnson, Harold 24
Johnston, Donny 215, 217
Ch. Juban's Georgia Jazz 208
Jubilo *(prefix)* 186
Jubilo Madcap 186
Jurkiewicz, Dee 31
Jurkiewicz, deForest F. 209, 210
Juvenile Cataracts 17, 165

K

Kalstone, Shirlee . . . . iv, 92
Kamps, Harriet 31
Kamps *(prefix)* 31
Ch. Kamps' Kaptain Kool 79
Ch. Kamps' Kountry Kiss 227, 228
Kane, Diana 204
Kaplan, Alice & Sheldon 86
Kaplar *(prefix)* 31, 169, 170
Ch. Kaplar's Jiminey Kricket 169, 208
Ch. Kaplar's Kelly Girl 170
Ch. Kaplar's Koka Kola 169
Ch. Kaplar's Kolleen 170, 227
Ch. Kaplar's Kwik-Kopi 216
Ch. Kaplar's Royal Kavalier 169
Ch. Kaplar's Quicksilver 170
Karcher, Mrs. Corinne C. 192
Kelley, Susan 111
Kellerhouse, Ken & Muriel 217
Kinschsular, Mike 204
Kirtland, Mr. & Mrs. George 181
Kittredge, David L. 207
Klaiss, Ted 164
Klepp, Judith Wick 207
Kobler, Dr. H.B. 22
Kraeuchi, Mr. & Mrs. L.C. (Ruth) 30

L

Lady Melissa D'La Swanson 148
Lady Rebecca D'La Swanson 148
Laffoon, William A. ("Tubby") 187
Lakeland Terrier 35
Lancaster *(prefix)* 185, 186
Ch. Lancaster Landmark 185
Ch. Laurim's Tri Performance 209
Ch. Laurim's Star Performance . . 221, 227, 228
Lazy Bend Kennels 188
Lee-ebs Sweetie Pie 184
Levy, Bob & Vivian 188, 189
L'Hommedieu, Mrs. 181
Ch. Limestone Laddie 22
Lincoln, Abraham 175
Little Buff Specially Me 171
Little, Dr. C.C 78
Log O'Cheer *(prefix)* 27

Ch. Low Desert Thanks a Million 227, 231
Ch. Lucknknow Creme De La Creme 20
Ch. Lurola's Lookout 197
Ch. Lydgate's Golden Girl 227, 232

M

Ch. Maddie's Vagabond Return . . 54, 184, 190, 194
Maida, Mr. Bob 132
Main-Dales Marathon Man 197
Ch. Makkell's Ziegfeld Girl 203, 217
Maplecliff *(prefix)* 27
Marks, Dr. & Mrs. Lewis Hart 27
Ch. Mar Lee's Folly O'Blarney 128
Marquez, Vernon & Karen 168, 169, 204
Marquis *(prefix)* 169
Ch. Marquis It's The One 168, 169
Ch. Marquis Mistletoe 227, 232
McCarr, Mr. & Mrs. Thomas 157
McCoy, Arch T. & Dorothy ("Dottie") . . 169, 205
McGrew, H.C. 145
McTavey, Harry 24
McTavey, Henry 19
Mellen, Col. William 137
Mellenthin, Herman 19, 22, 23, 24, 25, 30, 144, 154, 157, 158, 159, 174-176
Ch. Melodie Lane Mystique, UDT 123, 126, 127
Memoirs *(prefix)* 195, 196
Mepal *(prefix)* 22
Mepal's Fortunata 22
Merlady *(prefix)* 194
Merlyn's Jasper of Camelot, CDX 130
Ch. Merryhaven Strutaway 196
Ch. Merry Monarch of Falconhurst 23
Midbrook *(prefix)* 24
Ch. Midkiff Miracle Man 20
Ch. Midkiff Seductive 19
Miller, Lauren 154-155
Ch. Miller's Esquire, CDX 154
Ch. Miller's Peachie 155
Ch. Misty Wood JP TLC Miss Photogenic . . 214
Moffit, Ella B. 7, 9, 10, 139-141, 158, 173
Moffit, Mrs. A. R. 19
Moffit's Rowcliffe Diana 141
Monks of New Skete 131
Moon, Jerry 207
Ch. Mr. Holmeric 25
Murphy, Tommy 157
Muschal, Mrs. Ronnie 206
My Own *(prefix)* 22, 157
Ch. My Own Again 23
Ch. My Own Brucie 19, 20, 23, 24, 158, 159, 178

Ch. My Own Desire 175
Ch. My Own High Time. 144, 145, 154
Ch. My Own Peter Manning 175
Ch. My Own Peter The Great. 155
Ch. My Own Straight Sale 23, 175
Ch. My Own To-Day 19
Ch. Myroy Masterpiece 189
Ch. Myroy Night Rocket 189

N

Nash, Charles 206
Neilson, Howard Stout 144
Nelson, Roy. 187
New York Evening Sun 25
Noble Sir 181, 182
Nonquitt (*prefix*) 180, 181
Ch. Nonquitt Nola's Candidate 20, 25, 26,
   180, 181
Ch. Nonquitt Notable 181
Ch. Nonquitt Notable's Candidate 181
Ch. Nonquitt Nowanda 185
Norbill's High and Mighty. 171
Nor-Mar (*prefix*). 30, 165, 166
Ch. Nor-Mar's Nujac 166

O

Obedience Dog. 109, 119, 121, 125, 128,
   133, 136
   Companion. 121
   Tracking. 121, 125-127
   Utility. 121, 124-126, 128, 137
   Training Manuals 131
   Kennels & Schools. 131-132
O'Brien, George F. & Mary Ann 215
O'Neal, Tom F. 30, 194, 195
Orient's It's A Pleasure 190, 221, 223

P

Palacheck, Charles 140
Palm Hill (*prefix*) 31
Ch. Palm Hill Caro-Bu's Solid Gold. 210,
   221, 223
Ch. Palm Hill's Mountain Ashe. 209
Ch. Palm Hill's Starlet O'Hara. 227
Ch. Paradise's Blue Rebel Rouser 49
Payne, William T. 19
Pena, Pam Cullum 150
Petersen, William & Jean 31, 197, 198
Peuquet, Madeline E. 184
Pfrommer, Jim & Donna 169
Phillips, Dr. 78
Pike, Wilson 9
Ch. Pineshadows Coco Cub. 56
Pinetop (*prefix*) 187

Ch. Pinetop's Fancy Parade 187
Pinfair (*prefix*) 27
Am. Can. Ch. Eng. Sh. Ch. Piperhill's
   King Arthur 221, 225
Pitts, Mike & Linda. 205, 210
Poling's Royal Splendor. 184
Popular Dogs. 178
Ch. Pounette Fancy Dancer. 195
Pounette Perrette 195
Ch. Princess Marie . . . 20, 21, 23, 158, 175, 176
Professional Handlers Association (PHA) . . 31
Progressive Retinal Atrophy (PRA) 29
Proportion 42
   Forequarters 43
   Head. 42-43
   Hindquarters 44
   Neck, topline, body. 43
Puppy Mills. 32

Q

Q-Bush Happy Leroy, CDX. 149
Quackenbush, Marjorie L. 149

R

Red Brucie 22-24, 157, 158, 173-176, 183
Rees' Dolly. 22, 158, 174
Rees Latimer 22
Rees' Meteor. 22
Rendition (*prefix*). 172
Ch. Rendition Triple Play 172, 202
Ch. Rendition Silk Stockings 172
Rendle, Arthur E. 12
Rickertsen, Bryan C. & Marleen 206
Riggs, Lawrason 180
Ch. Rinky Dink's Robin 197
Ch. Rinky Dink's Sir Lancelot. . . . 31, 194, 197,
   221, 222
Rinky Dink's Smooth As Silk 197
Robbins, Billie. 123, 126, 127
Roberts, Anita 31, 167, 195
Robinhurst Foreglow 22, 158, 174, 175
Robinson, Kyle 207
Rosenbauer, Joy 124
Rosenbauer, Roy 137
Ross, Mrs. Henry A. 180-181
Rowcliff (*prefix*) 174, 175
F.T. Ch. Rowcliff Gallant 144
Ch. Rowcliff Princess 175
Ch. Rowcliff Red Man 175
Rowcliffe War Dance 140
Rowe, Charles & Jackie. 149, 208
Russ, Larry & Norma 217
Ch. Russ' Winter Beauty 217

S

Sabella, Frank 92
Sagamore *(prefix)* 164
Ch. Sagamore Toccoa. 164, 213
Saluki. 3, 39
Ch. Sandor's Coming Attraction, UDTX . . 127
Sandrex Sangarita. 169
Sand Spring *(prefix)* 175
Ch. Sand Spring Follow Through 159
Sand Spring Smile Awhile 181-182
Ch. Sand Spring Stormalong 160
Ch. Sand Spring Storm Cloud 20
Ch. Sand Spring Surmise 22
Ch. Saratoga's Secret Center 227, 228
Schmidt, Louis 184
Ch. Scioto Bluff's Judy. 190
Ch. Scioto Bluff's Sinbad 31, 173, 190, 194,
   221, 222
Ch. Seenar's Seductress 127, 227, 229
Seenar's Seraphin Sheaint, CDX/TDX 127
Self, Charles. 203, 206, 210
Ch. Shalimar's Soft Touch 227, 232
Ch. Sharob's Emerald Image 227
Sheila of Cassilis 22
Shiloh Dell *(prefix)* 30
Ch. Shiloh Dell's Salute 172
Shirl's Donnie-Mite, CD 122
Show Dog 91-118
   Grooming 95-96, 111-117
   Lead Training 104-108
   Posing 96
   Show Training. 92-93
   Sidewinding 108
   Sitting 108
   Size, standard 41
   Socialization 93-95
   Table Training. 95-96
   Temperament 109-110
Ch. Showtime Coronation Beauty 219
Shuey, Todd 137
Silver Maple *(prefix)*. 30
Ch. Showtime Classy Cheerleader. 218
Sir Blake the Gentleman, CD 137
Smith, Anthony. 1-2, 4, 6
Smith, Dr. & Mrs. Clarence 218
Smith, Julian & Ann 208
Smith, Myrtle 159
Ch. Sogo Showoff. 161
Spacht, Hugh & Marilyn. 31, 118, 207, 210
Stacy, Charlotte. 197, 198, 218
Stacy, Terry 198, 218
St. Andrea *(prefix)* 185
Ch. St. Andrea's Medicine Mane . 185, 186, 187
St. Andrea's Ragtime Gal 185, 187

St. Andrea's Rainmaker 185, 187
Steiner, Kim 130
Ch. Stobie's Service Charge 164
Stockdale *(prefix)* 26, 159, 172, 181
Stockdale Dinah 159
Ch. Stockdale Red Rocket 160, 189
Ch. Stockdale Startler. 160, 182
Stockdale The Great 160
Ch. Stockdale Town Talk. 24, 26, 160, 181,
   182, 183, 189, 221, 225
Stonehedge *(prefix)* 195
Stylish Pride 139
Sugartown *(prefix)* 27
Super Daddy. 169
Suplee, Mrs. 182
Swalwell, Arline 27, 56
Swanson, Pat. 148
Sweet Georgia Brown. 176

T

Tabaka, Ruth N. 129, 153, 219
Ch. Tabaka's Tidbit O'Wynden, CDX . . 129, 219
Ch. Tabaka's T. Tissue Tucki, CDX. 129
Ch. Tamara's All That Glitters. 227, 229
Ch. Tedwin's Lady Petite 154
Tedwin's Tale 171
Ch. Tedwin Tommy Tucker 154
Ch. Terje's Thunderbolt 210
The Cocker Southern 166
The Cocker Spaniel 7, 10, 173
The Cocker Spaniel Visitor 166
Ch. The Great My Own 20, 23
The Wagging Tail 166
Ch. Tompark's Little Rock. 51
Ch. Tonclee's Special Valentine. 168
Top Dog Exhibit 136-137
Torohill *(prefix)* 23, 176
Torohill Tidy 176
Ch. Torohill Trader. . . . 20, 21, 23, 24, 176, 177
Torohill Trouper 176
Totton, Arthur 178, 180
Towne, Wanda 104
Tracey 195
Ch. Tri Pod's Firefly 227, 229
Trojan *(prefix)* 86
Ch. Try-Cob's Candidate 25, 178, 179, 180
Ch. Try-Cob's Favorite Girl 20, 25
Try-Cob's Suzie Q 26
Twelvetrees, Mrs. Myrtle 187

V

Ch. Valli-Lo's Jupiter 171
Vanderveer, Dorothy. 192
Van-Dor Fancy Triane. 192

Ch. Van-Dor Vermillion 169
Van Horn, Evelyn Monte. 147
Van Ingen, Mrs. H. Terrel 27, 159
Van Meter, C.B. 26, 30, 160, 162, 182, 183

W

Wall, Mrs. Constance. 24
Wall, Mrs. Robert W. 182
Ch. Walltan's Show N' Tell 227
Ward, Calvin E.. 203
Washington, George 175
Washington State University . . 29, 31, 165, 209
Wegusen, Bea 30, 162, 190
Weiss, Amy & Lou . . 31, 119, 126, 198, 199, 202
Ch. Wendadam's White Shoulders. 227
Westminster Kennel Club 19, 25, 26, 31,
    159, 183
Whiting, Mary 128
FT Ch. Wildacre Harum Scarum. 145
Wilmerding, Clinton 11-15, 139, 141
Winders, Charles D. & Veda L. 190
Windridge *(prefix)* 27, 56
Windsweep *(prefix)* 19, 23, 175
Ch. Windsweep Ebony Boy 20
Ch. Windsweep Ladysman. 20, 23, 24, 177

Windy Hill *(prefix)* 31, 166, 167, 195, 196
Ch. Windy Hill's Eagle Scout. 167
Ch. Windy Hill's Makes-Its-Point. . . . 167, 196
Ch. Windy Hill's 'N Dur-Bet'Tis Patti 172
Ch. Windy Hill's 'Tis Demi's Demon. 31,
    167, 172, 195, 221, 224
Ch. Windy Hill's 'Tis Demi-Tasse. 196
Ch. Windy Hill's 'Tis Lipton's Rebuff. 227
Wise, Major Ivan & Dr. Paula 186
Wood, Dee Dee. 168, 169, 216
Wood, Frank & Dee Dee 205, 216
Wood, Frank. 147, 205
Wood, Marnie 137
Wright, Jeff 5, 199, 210
Wuchter, George 27
Wunderlich, Bill. 185

Y

Yakely, William L., DVM 29, 165
Young, Ted, Jr. . . 19, 31, 162, 206, 207, 217, 219
Young, Ted, Sr 154

Z

Zolezzi, John & Dawn 204